THE ALLURE OF ELSEWHERE

ALSO BY KAREN BABINE

Water and What We Know: Following the Roots of a Northern Life

All the Wild Hungers: A Season of Cooking and Cancer

THE ALLURE
OF ELSEWHERE

A Memoir of Going Solo

KAREN BABINE

MILKWEED EDITIONS

Published 2025 by Milkweed Editions

Printed in Canada

Cover design by Mary Austin Speaker

Author photo by Brandi Ashman

25 26 27 28 29   5 4 3 2 1

First Edition

Library of Congress Cataloging-in-Publication Data

Names: Babine, Karen, 1978- author.
Title: The allure of elsewhere / Karen Babine.
Description: First edition. | Minneapolis, Minnesota : Milkweed Editions,
   2025. | Includes bibliographical references. | Summary: "A memoir about
   camping alone in a Scamp camper and traveling to Nova Scotia to better
   understand her family's past"-- Provided by publisher.
Identifiers: LCCN 2024032972 (print) | LCCN 2024032973 (ebook) | ISBN
   9781571311825 (paperback) | ISBN 9781571317544 (ebook)
Subjects: LCSH: Babine, Karen, 1978- | Babine, Karen, 1978---Family. |
   Babine, Karen, 1978---Travel. | Babin family. | Nova Scotia--Genealogy.
   | Acadia--Genealogy. | Acadians--Genealogy. | Single
   women--Travel--Canada. | Recreational vehicle camping--Canada. |
   Minnesota--Biography.
Classification: LCC F1036.8 .B33 2025 (print) | LCC F1036.8 (ebook) | DDC
   929.20971--dc23/eng/20241205
LC record available at https://lccn.loc.gov/2024032972
LC ebook record available at https://lccn.loc.gov/2024032973

Milkweed Editions is committed to ecological stewardship. We strive to align our book production practices with this principle, and to reduce the impact of our operations in the environment. We are a member of the Green Press Initiative, a nonprofit coalition of publishers, manufacturers, and authors working to protect the world's endangered forests and conserve natural resources. *The Allure of Elsewhere* was printed on acid-free 100% postconsumer-waste paper by Friesens Corporation.

for my father

Let me essay, O Muse! to follow the wanderer's footsteps;—
Not through each devious path, each changeful year of existence,
But as a traveler follows a streamlet's course through the valley:
Far from its margin at times, and szeeing the gleam of its water
Here and there, in some open space, and at intervals only;
Then drawing nearer its banks, through sylvan glooms that conceal it,
Though he behold it not, he can hear its continuous murmur;
Happy, at length, if he find the spot where it reaches an outlet.

—Henry Wadsworth Longfellow, *Evangeline*

To know your history is to carry all your pieces, whole and shattered,
through the wilderness. And feel their weight.

—Sabrina Orah Mark

Author's Note

In this narrative, I've adopted a superscript numbering system to denote the generational lineage of family members, allowing readers to easily track familial relationships and connections throughout the story. A six-greats grandfather will have a superscript 6 next to their name, a nine-greats grandmother will have a 9. This choice aims to unclutter the sentences, while navigating through the intricate web of familial ties, particularly in stretches of my family history where it seems like everybody is cleverly named Pierre.

The name is Babin up until my three-greats grandparents' generation, when it acquired its final e. I don't know when the pronunciation changed from the soft French pronunciation of Babin to the long vowels of Babine, the first syllable *bay* as in *Bay* of Fundy, the second syllable as in L'Acadie Blanc *wine*.

INTRODUCTION

THE YEAR I TURNED THIRTY, I WAS TEACHING IN OHIO, and as was my habit, I went home to Minnesota for the summer break. My sister Kristi was getting married. Just for fun, Dad drove three hours south to meet me in Minneapolis, because I wanted to look at campers, and when you live in northern Minnesota you do things like drive three hours just for fun, and we worked our way up through the various RV dealers along Highway 10 north toward my hometown of Nevis. We finally ended up in Backus, at the Scamp factory, where they make the small, bulbous fiberglass campers that I'd wanted for years, maybe even half my life if I wanted to count back. Scamps are one of several kinds of lightweight molded fiberglass campers, and somebody once told me that the cult of Scamp is just as annoying as the cult of Apple: once you get one, you can't stop talking about it, and you never go back. You're Scamp for life. They're not wrong.

But things felt different that summer.

Maybe it was the cliché of my approaching thirtieth birthday in October.

Maybe it was something about turning thirty cutting down on people asking when I'd get married or have kids, convinced I'd change my mind, but I'd still say *I might find Mr. Right, but he's still going to have to live next door.*

Maybe it was that our concept of family and what that looked like was changing, all in good ways. Kristi married Mike that summer, they'd bought a house, and my youngest sister Kim moved in, the three of them creating an intentional community based on the idea that if and when Kim partnered, he'd move in, rather than her moving out. My tight-knit family was getting tighter. When my niece was born, I was incredibly grateful for Skype collapsing the distance between Ohio and Minnesota, even as Kristi's dog would look at my face on the screen, then worriedly look under the table, wondering where the rest of my body was. My parents moved down to the Twin Cities when they retired to be a much closer part of their grandchildren's lives instead of retiring to the Cabin in northern Minnesota as they had intended. We were still close, but there's a difference between visiting family and being close enough to show up for dinner on a whim. And I was still in Ohio, or Nebraska, or North Dakota, and *not there.*

Through my twenties, it was clear just how much the world is not set up for solo people, not emotionally or logistically. I came to dread the singles' table at friends' weddings, the kids' table at the California Grandparents' house, even as Kristi and Mike were permitted to sit at the adults' table because they were married and I wasn't, even though I was two years older. There weren't enough people at home to need a kids' table, so it was strange to be separated from the older generations until I'd achieved something I didn't know I was supposed to be pursuing. Everything about the world told me my life would only have value once I married, once I had kids, once I *grew up*, once I *settled down*. By the time I turned thirty, I was really tired of it. In August, back in Ohio to start a new school year, I found my perfect Scamp for sale in Cleveland and within a few days, it was sitting in my driveway.

In the years before the Scamp, working toward what it meant to be a solo woman in the world, I started traveling alone to Ireland, because travel—and solo travel specifically—helped me question these ready-made narratives that were so loud in my twenties, the expectations of marriage and children and the life I was supposed to lead, because that was just *how it was done.* What I loved most about those early-aughts trips to Ireland—about learning how to travel, why I wanted to travel, why I wanted to travel alone, why movement itself felt important—was noticing where my instinct to say *yes* faded into *no* and where *no* expanded into *why not?* Traveling alone is a thing apart, though, and traveling alone while female is another thing entirely. On my study abroad in 2000 when I was twenty-one, without any of those skills in place, I brought a huge hiker's backpack so comically big and heavy that I couldn't lift it into the overhead compartment by myself, with two giant suitcases that barely fit in the trunk of the taxi that would take us from the bus station to student housing. It was my first real lesson in self-sufficiency, in the style and determined enthusiasm of a toddler: *I need to do it by myself.* When I returned in 2005, my pack was half the size. In later years, I've gone even smaller just because I like the challenge.

But a *solo woman traveling* has been handed a Hollywood-ish story framework, established tropes of how a woman traveling alone must be afraid, or lost, or brash, or a lesbian, or not a lesbian, or stuck, or unable to change a tire, or sexy while skillfully changing a tire. The travel journey required of women—as popularly presented—must be away from a love interest, toward a love interest, toward healing, away from a toxic environment, presumably toward a fuller understanding of identity. So many of these stories are stories of escape, of being in search of oneself or rediscovering oneself, but none of those applied to me. I went alone, back to Ireland, for the simple reason that I wanted to. What was I waiting for? A very good question. I certainly didn't travel to go find myself because I'd never lost myself. It seemed an inherently silly proposition. I wasn't traveling in search of my identity or my place in the world because my family had already built that. I knew who I was, and I knew who I was in the context of my family. Who I was as an individual, I'd constructed that with my own hands, with the tools in my Craftsman tool bag that had been a gift from my father.

Last New Year's, he handed me a set of small Craftsman screwdrivers and said, *Santa forgot one.*

I grinned at him. *Do they come with fully functional legs so they can sprout and walk away from my tool bag, or do I have to install them myself?*—because it's a running joke for our tools to sprout legs and walk away so that we can never find them.

Dad grinned back. *They come ready to go.*

Fantastic, I said.

There are two types of stories common among families: one tells the story of *movement away*—from pain, from a life unwanted. The other is the *movement toward*—curiosity, adventure, making a name, separating yourself from an established story and figuring out who you are outside of it. There's something compelling about bone-deep curiosity as a reason for leaving and going elsewhere. There's a reason why *The Odyssey* is a story that can be retold on the streets of Dublin or in the banjo twang of *O Brother, Where Art Thou?* The best of these stories are roads on which we can write our own experience. When I started to question the path I'd been on and how it had created the person I saw in the mirror in the morning, it felt natural to keep taking steps backward even as my desire for travel moved me forward. One step leads to another step, something the ancient Chinese philosophers knew well, though I'd be surprised if they had a road trip in mind. Maybe they did.

———

FIVE YEARS LATER, TWO DAYS AFTER MY THIRTY-FIFTH birthday, my Minnesota grandmother Phyllis died, and suddenly our family lost a bright guiding spark, a foundational force. My grandfather Kermit had passed away in 2006, and our family of Minnesota Babines + my mother's parents, a solid little family of seven now reduced to five, was shrinking in ways that felt deeper than simply the loss of two people who were responsible for much of how our little family functioned and what we valued. Now they were both gone: Gram, who would recite the first stanzas of James Russell Lowell's "The First Snowfall" every time it snowed, and Grandpa, who taught us how to know how old a white pine is by counting its rings of branches.

Gram had left my sisters and me a little money, and it seemed prudent to save it for something important.

You should take a trip, my sisters said at some point that winter.

I could, but it feels frivolous.

Why? they asked. *Gram loved to travel. She would have loved to see you use it for that.*

I guess that was true, even though it felt like I should save it for a rainy day. I'd been in grad school living on a pittance of a stipend, so spending money of any sort felt vaguely wrong, but because of my financial situation, I'd barely used my Scamp for a couple of years. *If I were going to go on a big Scamp trip, where would I go? What would be a good use of this money that's suddenly made things possible— something that would make Gram look at me, smile that proud smile, and nod her head like she would do?*

I decided to point the Jeep and Scamp in the direction of my father's family, east toward Nova Scotia and the Canadian Maritimes. That's where the Babines, who were French-Acadian, came from back in the early days of Acadie in the 1620s, before *le Grand Dérangement* in 1755, when the English deported more than ten thousand French Acadians from the place they called Acadie, dumped them on ships bound for anywhere else, and the British renamed it Nova Scotia. I didn't know if this trip to Nova Scotia would turn out to be anything more than accumulating miles and new souvenir keychains, maybe discovering an affection for some geographically specific food that would spark nostalgia every time a certain pattern of weather crosses my day, but I think there was a part of me that didn't care which way I went, because I just wanted to do *something*. I was feeling restless about staying put too long.

As the family historian, I spend a lot of time wondering about the stories we *can* tell, the ethics of storytelling, of family secrets, of family pain, things that are not exactly secret, but things we choose not to talk about anyway. For some it might be an intellectual question—or not even a question at all—but for me, it's a really important question. The storyteller, the family historian, holds immense power and I feel the need to be careful, because stories aren't neutral. What I do with them will echo.

———

As I planned the trip, I taped quotes from W. Scott Olsen above my computer as I calculated miles and stopping points: "There is a pull to the universe, an insistent something that calls us out, then across. On the road, there is always the chance that the world will be unmade for us, then remade larger," and "What do we want from the viewed surface of the earth, from the way the earth rises and falls away, or doesn't? What do our hearts tell us we need from the shape of the land?" It felt good to read—and be reminded—that I didn't need to go elsewhere, to more important places, to know something true and real. Growing up in rural northern Minnesota, the only radio stations we could get were country and it felt good to sing along to our stories and lives, lakes and trees and dirt roads and Brad Paisley's "Ticks" and The Chicks' "Wide Open Spaces" and Little Big Town's "Boondocks," music that celebrated the place where we were, rather than the allure of elsewhere. I've lost a lot of interest lately in contemporary country music with women turned into objects and cruelty wrapped in patriotism, preferring instead to turn on blues, or bluegrass, from Trampled by Turtles to I'm With Her to The Wailin' Jennys and Red Molly and let those strings set fire to the air in a way that clears everything from here to the horizon. It feels good to sing your place in the world sometimes.

With different colored highlighters, I marked locations on the map from my family tree—Halifax, Yarmouth, Grand-Pré—and then worked my way backward while also working forward. At some point my lines would meet in the middle. Leaving Minneapolis, Thunder Bay, Ontario, seemed a good first-night stop, being about six hours away. There weren't any good places to stop between Thunder Bay and Sault Ste. Marie, so I resigned myself to an eight-hour drive. Sault Ste. Marie to Driftwood Provincial Park in Stonecliffe, Ontario, then onto Quebec City, Quebec. From there, Fredericton, New Brunswick, en route to Fundy National Park, where I'd spend a couple of days before heading up to Prince Edward Island. I wouldn't expect to encounter anything Babine until I left Prince Edward Island and headed for Halifax, but it seemed silly to get that close to Anne of Green Gables and not visit. I'd spend about ten days in Nova Scotia, then to Kennebunk, Maine, where the Babines settled for only a generation and a half before the family split and my great-grandparents headed for California. It would take me about four days from there to get back to Minnesota.

There are stories of women traveling, but few of them are road trips. We have early travel narratives by ship, tales of settler women making their way across the Great American Desert in wagons, and countless stories of walking. The road story of women is worth telling—and the camping stories of solo women equally so. Camping alone is the only time I have to be what feels like fully myself, fully immersed in the solitude I seem to need to function best. When I tell people I camp alone, so many wonder if I get lonely, but the truth is that I almost never am. I might text *wish you were here* to my family, and it's just as easy to text friends a picture, and that seems to satisfy the need to share a moment with another human being. I'm alone, I'm solitary—but I'm not disconnected. My connections to people and the world are vibrant and strong. I just like coming home to an empty house where I can recharge my social battery in peace.

It feels deliberate and methodical, the way that I never pursued permanent partnership or kids, and while I'm not opposed to partnership, the act of changing my mind would have to include significant effort. I have a house, a job, and a full life. *He's not competing with other men to be with me*, I'd think, *he's competing with me*, and I like my life just the way it is. Even if our decisions are based in a unique worldview, we make our choices out of curiosity, or stubbornness, out of external societal pressure. Sometimes I do things purely out of spite because I'm a Scorpio, but I also think there's a certain kind of stubbornness that is less obstinate and more just a function of immovability, the work of simply never changing course, and getting where you want to go simply because you never considered another option, never considered that the thing would not happen. It's a kind of stamina, the work of constructing a life by playing the long game, which requires a certain kind of emotional and mental endurance. It's not stubbornness, but that's the closest language I have.

The Scamp fell into this mindset too. I couldn't be talked into buying a camper that would sleep two or more people comfortably or that would fit a dog I didn't have. I always wanted the Scamp, way back at the beginning, back when we'd occasionally see them when we went camping when I was young, and it never occurred to me to choose a different camper—or even that I wouldn't have one at some point in my life. It was a kind of inevitability that didn't feel so much stubborn, as *of course it is*. If Mr. Right ever showed up, we'd renegotiate the camper situation—in the meantime, I wasn't going to live my life for somebody who may or may not ever exist. Even then, I might still keep the Scamp and go camping by myself.

When I'm at home, wherever home is, and the Scamp is parked in the driveway, sometimes I'll go out there, close the door behind me, lie down on the bed, and just take a deep breath. There's something elementally comforting about the interior shape of this tiny camper, how it feels so much larger on the inside than it does from the outside, something I assume has to do with the curved shape. When the world is just a little bit too much, I discard the shell of my house and take on the shell of the camper and let it form the physical barrier between me and the world, especially in times when what holds me together feels fragile, my skin feels thin, when my self feels like you could see through me. It's not a matter of spending time in the camper to remember who I am, but rather a matter of being reminded of the deliberate choices I've made to live my life the way I want to.

THE ALLURE OF ELSEWHERE

CHAPTER ONE

'M IN THE BACK SEAT OF A BLACK DIESEL BLAZER WITH my two younger sisters; Dad is driving, Mom is navigating. It's July 1987, and we're driving through the Mojave Desert to San Diego to visit Dad's family—the California Babines—and it's our first major travel together as a family, and we're learning the peculiarities and practicalities of what this kind of movement means. I'm eight, Kristi is six, Kim is four. We don't have air conditioning, because Dad just had the engine rebuilt, and since it was still getting broken in he's worried about the Blazer overheating—and in the middle of the Mojave Desert in temperatures past 100 degrees Fahrenheit and probably closer to 110 degrees—and so we try to make do with the windows rolled down. From an eight-year-old view, there is nothing to see, the world empty and spreading out beyond sight to a place where you're not sure if it's mirage or real. It is intensely miserable, the kind of misery that melts animosity between small girls who would prefer not to be sitting so close to each other, little legs imprinted with the rough cloth of the back seat, sticky skin scorched by metal seat belts that still somehow emotionally mark the 1980s on

1

my skin, bickering over which two of the three would get to use the two red tape players, who had to sit in the middle seat, and *she's touching me! No, I'm not! Yes, you are!*

We like telling the stories of how my sisters and I made up our own games on trips like these. There was the standard license plate game, which was always a little more fun when we hit national parks or stayed on Air Force bases, which is where we usually found Alaska and Hawaii. Once we got all fifty states, our reward was ice cream. I suspect we would have gotten ice cream anyway. Over the years, my sisters and I invented The Quote Game, which mostly consisted of somebody picking a movie, like *The Princess Bride*, and the first one not to be able to come up with a quote lost.

Have fun storming the castle!
Anybody want a peanut?
As you wish.

The first ones were easy, but once you got the easy ones out of the way, the quotes got more obscure, and the game got harder.

I was from a land of lakes and trees, so deserts were a curiosity—Petrified Forest and Four Corners, where we could stand in four states at once, and Mesa Verde where we dipped into the coolness of kivas and thrilled at what it would be like to live in that place and time—but on days like this, when little girls are too hot even to argue, the vast, open landscape is not interesting. It is simply space to move through en route to somewhere else. When we finally drive into Needles, California, our suffering is rewarded with Dairy Queen, where I still remember how the forty-degree change in temperature from outside to inside made me a little nauseous. Even now I can still feel that knowledge in my body, my belly, that memory, that place.

They were an exotic dream, this family of California Babines, the way people become in your imagination. We rarely got to see them, but we knew where they lived, because California was special. We saw it on television and in movies all the time. They lived just north of San Francisco, land of cable cars, sourdough, and Alcatraz. They drove the Golden Gate Bridge, ate See's candy and Ghirardelli chocolate. I grew up in small-town Minnesota, where our biggest claim to fame in Nevis was as the home of the World's Largest Tiger Muskie, and when people came to visit us, we took them twenty miles away to see the headwaters of the Mississippi River. We ate lefse and venison and wild rice. Everything that was important in the world was elsewhere, and not *here*. California—or the East Coast—was where a person went when they grew up, gained reason.

The California Babines we were going to see were a family to pin stories and hopes of stories on, because they were the aunts and uncles and cousins that I always wanted but didn't have in Minnesota, because my mom was an only child. There was a part of me that desperately wanted to belong to a large, boisterous family who had large, boisterous gatherings, energetic events of deep, generational memory-making, and my dad had three brothers and a sister, and they each had families full of cousins who were nearly the same age as my sisters and me. I always wanted best-friend cousins, the way I saw in my books. I was the oldest, and while Kristi, Kim, and I played together well, generally got along, and had great imaginations that led to epic adventures, sisters were not cousins. The life of the California Babines was the kind we read in books, stories we saw on television when we watched *Full House* on TGIF every Friday.

The allure of elsewhere. It was a concept I knew before I had words for it. When we went to stores, we could find giant framed photographs of New York, or Paris, or San Francisco—never the Minneapolis skyline or the Stone Arch Bridge. The stories I read were never set in Minnesota, and I wouldn't learn until college that the first American to win the Nobel Prize in Literature was a Minnesotan. High culture happened in New York or Los Angeles or Seattle or New Orleans, not St. Paul. *Elsewhere.* When Starbucks started its You Are Here mug series, I was irrationally excited to see the Twin Cities represented, but unless you specifically went to a local gift shop, you weren't going to find I ♥ Minneapolis or Gray Duck T-shirts.

The place I grew up in was the butt of jokes, full of unsophisticated people and bland food, with a football team whose blowing of a field goal in 1999 in the NFC Championship still causes Minnesotans acute pain. We haven't won a World Series since 1991, though the Twins did win the World Series in 1987 on my birthday. We had to laugh at ourselves. Everybody else did. Once I applied for a job on the East Coast, and they asked me in the interview if I'd ever lived in a city before—and I was living in Minneapolis at the time. California—and the West in general—was important. Everything I read told me so, even as I died of dysentery nearly every time I played *The Oregon Trail.* My mother learned not to name the game characters after her children.

In 1989, my parents bought a 1972 Starcraft pop-up, all army-green canvas and brown fake wood, and it became part of the core stories we created as a family of five Minnesota Babines. Mom went camping with her parents in a pop-up when she was a kid and she wanted to make those memories with us and Dad, too, had gone camping with his family when he was young, though my mother refused to sleep in a tent. They compromised on a pop-up. Camping became the cheapest way to get out to California to visit, because even though the California Grandparents visited every few years, none of my dad's siblings or their families would come east, and logistically I understand it's easier for five people to see a large group rather than the reverse. In the same way, these days it's easier for me as a solo person to travel to spend time with my family, given my teaching schedule in the summers allows for extended time up north.

We'd rented our friend's pop-up for two years and had really liked it, and one day my mother came home, full of five-foot-three-inch blonde excitement—"Dan, there's a pop-up for sale on the side of the road!"—and my parents jumped in the Blazer, drove over, and bought it on the spot. My parents were in their late thirties, younger than I am now, and full of the glee parents of young children have when they decide to start making a specific kind of memory with their kids. I can imagine their grins as they drove home, filled with the kind of anticipation that's specific to travel, to camping. My favorite family stories—the Minnesota Babines', that is—probably could be written on the interstates, in one big line, with the dotted median providing the guidelines to keep our penmanship confined, like in elementary school notebooks. This, I think, is not an accident. Even my parents' courtship—the first story of the Minnesota Babines, before we became so—is a road story. We could tell you stories about Dinosaur National Monument in Utah and six-year-old Kristi loudly declaring that she wanted to be an *alientologist* when she grew up, or how in riding the tram up, Kristi's pink Mickey Mouse hat, recently purchased at Disneyland, flew off and into the brush, and how my dad was a hero and walked down the mountain to get it back for her. We were forbidden to mention the *alientologist* incident for many years. I could tell you how hot it was the day we went to Arlington National Cemetery and the pictures show the three of us girls decked out in our fanny packs, Mickey Mouse hats, neon-yellow insulated water bottle holders embroidered with our initials, and bright plastic sunglasses.

We could tell you the story of the bison in Yellowstone, where the boys across the road antagonized a bull so thoroughly that he, incandescent with rage, thundered into the thicket of brush next to our campsite, shredded the brush with his horns, then stomped into our campsite, several tons of justifiably enraged creature, snorting with the deep, bad-tempered annoyance that only bison can manage. I don't remember where Mom and Dad were, but Kristi was outside, Kim and I inside the camper. The bison stared at Kris for a while, then he took a giant bison-sized dump near enough to the awning stake that we nearly *had to dig it out*, as the story goes, and ambled toward the next campsite, where a group of teenage girls had been laughing at us. The bison knocked their tabletop grill off the table, licked it clean, then proceeded to scratch an itch on his hump on the side of their pop-up camper, rocking it off its jacks, while the girls muffled screams. We got the last laugh.

These stories of our family's travel and camping, of Lake Superior and Winnipeg and the Badlands and Washington, DC, but especially the ones on the road to California, form some of my own core stories. *How do those stories become core?* Is it in the accumulations of telling, like how snow becomes ice becomes a glacier that moves and shapes mountain valleys? Our story as a family of Minnesota Babines is no more complicated than *we're a family who actually likes each other*—but we were also a family that was often in pursuit of family, putting tires to road so that we could spend a couple of weeks standing inside our own history, our own stories.

It felt like the California Babines, somewhere along the line, decided to impose the atrophying silence of *don't speak unless spoken to* on their descendants, cutting us all off from the ancestry of who we used to be. My grandfather rarely spoke about his family, preferring to tell stories about the present, and my grandmother and her sister didn't get along, so we learned not to ask any questions about how they celebrated their birthdays as kids or what their favorite Christmas present was or when they learned to ride a bike, because *children should be seen and not heard.*

I once said this to my sisters, and Kristi pointed out that Grandpa never stopped talking, which was true. Dad said, *Grandpa talked about things he enjoyed, things he was interested in. He told stories about things that gave him an identity. He wasn't really interested in conversation. He talked about being the parts manager at the Chevy dealer and rebuilding his 1941 Chevy pickup, because knowing everything there was to know about cars gave him an identity. He liked to talk about camping with Mom because he knew what to do and how to do it, and he liked being an expert about things. If you wanted to know anything about roses or cars or plumbing, you asked Bill Babine.* It made sense, that the way my grandfather thought about himself and his place in the world was constructed with his own hands, his own effort, his own brain. He wasn't who he was because of who his parents or extended family made him.

In my memory, Grandpa didn't tell stories, but the reality is he told the same three stories about his past, whether it was building an adobe house he'd grow up in in Ramona with his father, Bill Sr., and twin brother, Walt, in the late 1930s—a house that Zillow is now valuing at nearly $700,000—or getting accidentally left in Kansas with his brother when the family was driving cross-country in 1930. He'd tell my dad the story of his Uncle Dave—a name that appears nowhere in his ancestry, so I assume it was a family friend—who had homesteaded in Ramona because the land was cheap and Bill Sr., my great-grandmother Catherine, Grandpa, and Walt moved down there not long after. I can't find anything more about who Dave might have been, but it must have been someone important, given that Walt named his eldest son David. Embedded in those stories about building the adobe house was an element of being an expert, which, as Dad pointed out, gave my grandfather an identity, a place in the world, a certain kind of value.

Here's what I keep coming back to: How do I reconcile the reality that my grandfather was always talking, but my perception of deep silence remains? Certainly there's a kind of speech that fills a room with sound to its very corners, in between dust motes, into the cracks in the ceiling, but manages to say nothing at all. Grandpa talked; we listened. He might talk about how to prune roses and what you needed to make them grow so tall and lush, how he and Marion collected vases from thrift stores, filled them with roses from his garden and brought them to shut-ins and sick friends from church. He might tell us all about how to change the color of hydrangeas, whose color was dependent on the pH of the soil—and how he dumped a handful of nails near their roots and that's why he had the colors he did. (Turns out the nails have nothing to do with changing the pH of the soil, but one did not correct him.) And if nobody could contribute to the conversation, if our role was simply to sit, perhaps that's where my perception of silencing comes from. It's something I continue to wrestle with because I want to believe that both things can be true.

As I learned more about the family history, the dark times that deserve quiet, I would learn there were understandable reasons for what felt like California Babine silence about how we came to be who and where we were in the world, war and death and pain and historical trauma in our recent and ancestral past, but I didn't know how far back along the road of family history I would need to go to find where the California Babines ultimately decided what mattered were the stories they created themselves in the present, for the future. Nothing would be gained by engaging with or questioning the past.

My grandmother Marion never had much to say about her own parents, other than a deep dislike of her father, so getting more from her was impossible. The same was true of my grandfather. I want to know their stories of growing up in San Diego, what it was like for them when their kids were little. I want to know the smell of Santa Ana winds and the flavor of earthquakes, how that affected the way the California Babines lived their lives, how they arranged their shelves, how they always kept a milk can of water right outside the back door in case of fire, or other stories I've made up for myself in the absence of real ones.

I'VE BEEN THE FAMILY HISTORIAN SINCE I WAS SEVENTEEN, the day I walked into my dad's office with my childishly sketched family tree and asked him about an anomaly I'd found: his grandmother Catherine and uncle Walt shared the same death date. I remember asking if it had been a car accident, because I'd never heard anyone talk about them.

My dad picked it up, studied it. "No," he said, and I didn't expect the answer to be *murder*.

He told me that a month before he and my mother got married in 1976, his cousin David had a schizophrenic break and beat their grandmother and his own father, my father's uncle and grandfather's twin brother, to death. The weapon was a ring sizer—David was making jewelry at the time—and Dad used his hands to show me the shape of the thing.

Until that moment, I'm not sure I knew my grandfather had a brother, let alone a twin, and certainly nobody had ever talked about them, alive or dead. As I thought about it later, I wondered about what else I didn't know about the family history and the consequences of not knowing. Maybe I could have picked my great-grandmother Catherine off the family tree, but in hindsight, I can't be sure I knew about Walt. Maybe this shouldn't have been surprising; my very elegant and proper grandparents were very much a *children should be seen and not heard* household, and they didn't talk about much of substance when we were around, but to some extent I understand that they wouldn't talk about such things around young children. That's understandable.

The light was so bright in my dad's office with its east and south exposures, the west wall lined with handmade oak bookshelves made by an old German cabinetmaker in the church. Dad, sat in the L created by his large oak desk and black plastic computer table, turned his chair and looked at me across the desk. I sat on the floral love seat, which was so stiff as to be uncomfortable, but he had explained once that it was easier for old people to get out of than one that was more squishy. Dad was in his late forties, his hair still more pepper than salt.

Where were you? I asked.

Abilene. I got emergency leave from the Air Force and flew out the next day.

I stared at him, not sure what to say.

David was found not competent to stand trial, and he's spent the rest of his life in a prison mental hospital, he said. David died there in 2023.

I didn't tell your mother where I was going and got in a lot of trouble for it, but she understood once I explained.

I nodded carefully, sitting very still, as if restless movement in the listening was disrespectful somehow. I remember this feeling, almost like my dad's memory—coming out of what was, on its surface, an innocuous question—was predatory, like it had somehow triggered a freeze reflex rather than fight or flight. I couldn't explain it, but I felt it.

My mother took charge of all the arrangements, he said, *and she didn't let my dad see the bodies. She took care of everything at the funeral home, the caskets, the funerals, everything.*

I tried to imagine all this, the aftermath of murder, especially a terrible double murder, the police, the autopsy, the funeral home, and instead I focused on my grandparents who were not yet my grandparents, trying to manage through an event that nobody should have to. Later I would truly understand how my grandparents' relationship was complete in itself, unaffected by other people, even their children or grandchildren. They were like two sides of a magnet, absolutely complete, bonded. From this angle, their love and their relationship was one to be deeply envied. I often think the best relationships are the ones where the participants make each other better as people—and that was certainly true of my grandparents. In some ways, the addition of children and grandchildren did not add to the fulfillment of their lives—I think they had children just because it's what you did after you got married, the default, but I could be wrong about that. In this moment now, as I'm trying and failing at imagining these terrible days, I'm grateful that they had each other in this way, and I can't fault them, or their reactions, at all. In hindsight, my grandmother taking such complete charge and shielding my grandfather from memories he didn't need to carry was a supreme act of love.

Dad was more clinical in the telling than I would have expected, the story delivered as if it had happened to some other family. I would have expected more emotion, more something, but maybe the human body does what it can to protect us from such deep hurt, to keep us safe, even decades later. As the family historian, I've sourced the data, the death certificates, letters, newspaper clippings with the details of what Walt's wife Sally found when she came home that Sunday evening. Some of it I will share if my family asks, but it's not easily voiced. It's not a trauma I carry in myself, but I'm close enough that I need to be careful how I talk about it. It's not secret, but it is private—but even so I continue to question what's at stake if we don't talk about it, at least within the family.

My dad said, *We buried my grandmother next to my grandfather in Escondido, and I asked my dad if he would come back and visit their graves, and he said he wouldn't. "If I didn't tell them I loved them in life,"* he said, *"it makes no sense to do it now."*

As a kid, this felt really profound—and it hasn't changed much in the time since. *If I didn't tell them I loved them in life, it makes no sense to do it now.*

If I were to trace my origin story as the family historian, it would come back to this moment: a curious teenager, bright afternoon sunshine, the blond oak of my dad's desk at the small-town church where he was a pastor, my memory geographically located in this *here* and this *now*.

You've written this down, right? my sisters will ask any time we talk about family history, and I will nod, eagerly, because being the family historian is satisfying in ways I have not yet been able to articulate. When the stories of a family are painful and they only exist in fragments, it feels like the obligation of the family historian to fill in the gaps where I can to complete the story. *How do you know this?* they will ask and I can point to newspapers that detail the aftermath of Walt and Catherine's deaths and what happened to David after, but part of my obligation includes the ethics of when to tell stories, when not to, and when silence is a kindness because I care deeply about the people left behind for whom these events will never be history. I constantly wrestle with the line between *what we will say among family* and *what we will not say among strangers*—because my position on that line is different from each of my family members, and it changes according to circumstances. Sometimes the silence we inherit influences our own, or at least mine.

I love every bit of this work, even the painful discoveries, from sorting through boxes of photographs and funeral bulletins to digging through Ancestry.com and discovering the death certificate for my great-grandmother Catherine, which includes her cause of death—homicide—as well as extensive notes on the nature of what caused her death. It's hard to read, impossible to say out loud. What I don't understand about it, though, is that it lists her burial at Oak Hill Cemetery in Escondido, which is not where her husband, Bill Sr., is listed as buried—and the mystery of it will lead from one thing to another until I find that they're both buried at Oak Hill Cemetery. Then I remember my dad's voice: *we buried her next to my grandfather in Escondido.* I don't have enough information to know if he was reinterred, but I'm glad they're together, at peace. I love the inferring and the assuming and the speculation of putting all this data into an order that tells a story, accumulating enough information that imagination can fill in the gaps in stories in a logical way, because these are real people, not simply names and dates. It feels really important to me and I have an intense need to take my dad's speculative and wistful *I'd like to go to San Diego and show all of you the adobe house* and book a plane ticket *now* so I can stand in that place with him and know something I couldn't know any other way.

I'm the one who remembers, so the family doesn't have to.

———

TWO MONTHS BEFORE I LEFT FOR NOVA SCOTIA, I WENT TO pick up the Scamp from winter storage at the county fairgrounds. I called ahead and gave the lady my name but knew that it would be more effective if I told her that *mine's the thirteen-foot Scamp.*

Oh! she said. *That's the cute one we all love!*

I drove up to the fairgrounds and saw my little white Scamp sitting there in all its bulbous, egg-shaped glory with two men in their fifties, dressed in tan Carhartt coveralls, waiting for me. *You're here to pick up the Snapper, aren't you?*

I grinned against the cold that sapped the dexterity from my fingers. *Yes,* I said, *yes, I am.*

As I pulled around to back the Jeep up to the Scamp, the men measured the distance between the stinger and the Scamp hitch with their hands, finally holding up a hand for me to stop.

Don't tell me I got it on the first try, I said, even though I knew I had. *Something* about being a solo woman camper makes me feel like I've got something to prove. Maybe I do. Maybe it's hard to still shake the stigma of being a solo woman in her thirties, a woman camping, the cultural construction of who I'm supposed to be at this point in my life. When I'm sitting in the driver's seat of the Jeep, especially if the Scamp is attached, I'm extra sensitive to jokes about women drivers.

The men deftly hooked up the Scamp, the safety chains, the wiring, almost before I'd gotten out of the Jeep. One of the men asked me if I had a bolt for the hitch lever.

Yes, I said, *it's in the camper.* The padlock and my heavy-duty bungee cord were on the dinette table where I'd left them six months ago. When one of the men saw that I had a padlock, he grinned at me.

Smart, he said to the other guy. *She's smart. Not just a bolt, but she's got a padlock to make sure it doesn't come off.*

I let the guys peek inside the Scamp, because they'd never seen another one—let alone seen inside one. They poked their head in, asked if the AC turned it into a Deepfreeze, marveled that it had a furnace, and decided between them that it was perfect for one person.

Yes, I said. *Yes, it is.*

I bet it pulls like a dream, one of them said.

I nodded. *Like a dream.*

CHAPTER TWO

I PULL OUT OF MY PARENTS' DRIVEWAY IN MINNEAPOLIS almost at the stroke of 9:00 a.m. on Memorial Day, with my parents trying to find the line between being helpful and being in the way. I'm using their house as my departure point to Nova Scotia, along the North Shore of Lake Superior to Thunder Bay, partly because their house is centrally located and partly so that my dad can help me with last minute fixes and tinkerings. My dad's love language is a language of the road; it's windshield wiper fluid and air in my tires and that gas-line antifreeze stuff in the winter that I never think of. He's been carrying on a love affair with seat belts for decades, ever since he wrecked his 1968 International Scout on winter roads when I was two weeks old, which led to my mother strapping a newborn into the car to go get him while the roads were bad enough to wreck the truck with four-wheel drive.

She was maaaad at you, I say.

She was, Dad agrees, ruefully.

The replacement vehicle, a 1972 Scout, only came with front seats, and he sourced the back seat and other fripperies from the local junkyard, and it was full of all kinds of things he could find a use for. He sewed a holder for his Thermos that's still being used nearly forty years later and straps for his camper leveling blocks. He had so many projects that my mother made him get his own sewing machine, because he kept wrecking hers. Where my dad had junkyards, I have thrift stores. It's the same concept—build your life the way you want it to look. And I like that his most useful construction material is meant to keep its occupants safe. If my parents' courtship is a road story, the story of my father's parenthood is a road story, too, of making sure his children are safe as they make their way about the world.

Dad helps me back up and hitch the Scamp but then leaves me to my final preparations. I secure the interior, loading it so there's more weight toward the tongue. Because it's only fifteen hundred pounds of lightweight fiberglass, rather than a heavier, more standard stick-built camper that we're more familiar with, the Scamp will flop around on the hitch if it's not loaded right. I make sure the cupboard doors are securely shut. Bungee cord the closet door closed because it likes to pop open. Take down the curtains on the front and back windows, so I can see straight through. These things have become so routine that I don't even register them anymore.

I accept Dad's assistance checking the electrical, because it's difficult to check whether the brake lights work on the camper without a second set of eyes.

Right blinker, he calls and I push the lever up.

Left blinker? I push the lever down.

Brakes? I press the brake pedal.

Lights? I turn the indicator.

Good! he calls, and I'm suddenly ten years old, feeling special as I sit in the driver's seat of whatever Blazer or Suburban we have at the time, checking the electrical on our pop-up. It was a job that my sisters and I traded, because the driver's seat was a grown-up place to be, but I feel like I did it more often than not. Sometimes I'd be the one at the back making the calls.

What I've learned from my dad is a larger lesson of being self-sufficient, the work of making a home and a life in a literal sense as well as figurative. It's looking at a problem not simply as a problem but as a chance to make your life function just a little bit more efficiently without having to rely on anyone else. It's why I laugh at narratives of "men, if you're going to date an independent woman, you need to be prepared" with video of women moving furniture by themselves, wrestling mattresses into place without assistance, managing their landscaping alone, and the advice that *she doesn't need you, she wants you,* and I think about the increasing independence of women and the deliberate choice to marry, or partner, or do neither. We don't need a partner to support us financially, because we can do it ourselves. We don't need a husband to get a mortgage or a credit card anymore, and I don't need anyone to open pickle jars for me, because I can do it myself. It's why I'm glad I know the basics of plumbing, enough to reach for Drano or YouTube, because I refuse to pay a plumber to look at me like I'm stupid. Even though I can depend on my family if I need them, I need to be able to manage my life on my own.

I think the concept of daughters baffled my dad for the longest time, down to changing diapers and learning that there's a right way and a wrong way to wipe. He was a boy from a family of boys, after all. After Kim was born, somebody at church asked my parents if they were going to keep trying for a boy. Another friend replied for them, deadpan, "Eh, the boys will be around soon enough."

What do you do with girls?—besides finding them delightful, because what's not to love about walking into church on
a Sunday to the chorus of *hi daddy hi daddy hi daddy* from the
front pew and having to say *good morning, girls* before greet-
ing the congregation? And then hoisting one of us on his hip
while he shakes hands with the parishioners as they walk out
of the church afterward? He learned how to make ponytails
because that's the only hairstyle I would wear, and he needed
the ones with plastic balls on the end, not the loops, because
his hands were too big to manage otherwise.

I have very early memories from when I'm about four
of sleepy Sunday afternoons while my mother and sisters
were still napping and snuggling up with Dad on the brown
plaid couch with an afghan in front of *MASH*, not realizing at the time that Hawkeye Pierce would become my
first crush, an imprinting of snark that never goes away.
When he's four, my nephew Sam, influenced by reruns of
Full House, will watch Gwyneth Paltrow in her short shorts
at the beginning of *Avengers* and say, reverently, under his
breath, *Haaave mercy!* I wonder about his imprinting too.

I was nine the first time I asked the Easter Bunny for
a Swiss Army knife, one like my dad carried in his pocket,
because I wanted to be just like my dad—only to be told
that the Easter Bunny dealt in Swiss chocolate, not Swiss
Army knives. Hawkeye might have been my first crush, but
MacGyver was my first love. When I finally got a Swiss
Army knife of my own, I made a survival kit out of a small
leather pouch that contained Tylenol, meat tenderizer for
bee stings, Band-Aids, waterproof matches, a tiny Maglite
flashlight, and other assorted things that might be useful
in an emergency, and I carried that thing everywhere for
years. I wanted to be prepared for anything. Now I carry a

small Leatherman multitool, even if the occasion calls for a fancy evening bag. When she is twelve, my niece Cora will ask my dad for a Buck knife for Christmas. I support this. Dad buys her a Buck knife and has it engraved with her name. She opens the present and bursts into tears. A few months later, when she turns thirteen, Dad gives her a rolling pin handmade by his brother, Uncle Dennis, a talented woodworker, to support her love of baking. I give her a Leatherman. This family raises well-rounded kids.

When I'm alone and checking the electrical myself, it's a three-step process: left blinker and walk around the back to check, then I pick up the chocks; on the second, right blinker and double-check the safety chains and the hitch lock; third time, turn on the lights, circle the camper and lock the door. At this point when I'm alone, I usually trust that if those lights are working, my brake lights are fine. It's a risk but unavoidable.

With everything in place and double-checked, I make my final goodbyes to my parents, strong hugs and our classic goodbye ritual warning of *watch out for deer and idiots*, and slowly pull out of their driveway. They stand in the driveway, my mother short and blonde, my dad tall and dark, waving, until I'm out of sight. It's a family ritual to wave away the departing, one that Kristi and Mike adopted from their friend Terra, which has morphed into my sisters calling to the kids, *Come dance Aunt Kinny away*. It feels vaguely wrong to go inside before someone is out of sight.

My cats have been in their kennels for a while and they're already irritated, not sure if it's worse to be left home or go with me. Galway's kennel goes into the passenger seat, Maeve behind the driver's seat. Galway is eleven and his idea of roughing it is a Super 8. He is not a fan of this Nova

Scotia plan. He's skeletally skinny, with black-and-gray tiger stripes, green-gold eyes, and a funky heart-shaped white spot on his spine. He was badly abused before I adopted him, and he retains deep fear of the world and an aversion to being touched, or startled, or disturbed in any way. His default facial expression is judgmental. Maeve is seven, a beautiful Siamese with bright blue eyes, and weighs somewhere between ten and twelve pounds. We tend to describe her as short legged rather than zaftig. She was originally intended for Gram, because we thought getting her a cat would be a good idea, as she'd recently lost her schnauzer, Muffy, to old age. We didn't take into account that Gram was on blood thinners and Maeve is evil. It lasted two weeks. I couldn't take her back to the shelter, so she joined my little family, much to Galway's intense disapproval. With Maeve, I can depend on the morning report when I get up, usually delivered at top volume and with maximum profanity. She is not a fan of this plan either.

There's always a moment right before shifting the Jeep into drive that feels significant, the moment of allure between being somewhere and not yet being somewhere else. It's a glorious day, bright sunshine, and *north* means something different on the road, more a concept than a destination or compass direction, and is it too much to say it's one of my favorite feelings, these tires, this road, this kind of moment, this joy of being in the driver's seat of my life, actively pursuing a curiosity with a dream attached to the hitch, attempting a new landscape without any real expectation of what I'll find or how I'll feel when I get there?

How to talk about anticipation? It's more than adrenaline in the blood, it's an intensity to the muscles around your eyes, it's W. Scott Olsen:

When you begin a road trip, there are things you believe. It's not a matter of choice. You believe, for example, that your destination will be there. You believe that the town or the city or the lake or the campsite will be where you last left it, or where you've been promised it waits. You do not wonder about asteroids, rapture, or the sudden strike of a nuclear war in an otherwise peaceful time. When you first turn the key and feel an engine's spark, when you put the car in a gear to begin, it would be too much to say that you're even worried about these things. Worry implies a perceived risk. Faith would be a better word. When you begin a road trip, faith that the world this day will be the one you know.

I pull onto Highway 169 north toward Highway 610, which will take me to I-35 north to Duluth, en route to Thunder Bay, Ontario.

One woman, two cats, three axles, and sixty square feet of dreams.

———

NORTHBOUND ON I-35, DECIDUOUS TREES GIVE WAY TO pines, and I largely tune out my peripheral vision in favor of concentrating on the road. Minnesota is home to three biomes—the prairies of the west and southwest where my grandfather comes from, the eastern temperate deciduous forests that form a stripe in the southeast and east-central where my grandmother comes from, and then the north-central and northeast are coniferous forests where my sisters and I grew up. Each of these places creates a different story for the people living there, even down to what they used to build their homes and what they ate for dinner. I'm driving through two of them today toward Thunder Bay, and I like knowing that.

I am acutely aware of pointing my Jeep in the direction of other people's stories, stories that I'm related to but are not mine, stories of love and loss and fear and family and politics and upheaval. I drive past Hinckley and think that maybe I should stop there sometime and walk into the stories of the 1894 Great Hinckley Fire, which burned more than two hundred thousand acres and killed almost five hundred people. The fire was so hot it melted the railroad tracks, as the story goes. I like audiobooks while I drive, so I've got on my favorite Larry Millett mystery, *Sherlock Holmes and the Red Demon*, which puts Sherlock Holmes and Watson in Minnesota on the trail of an arsonist before he starts a fire in Hinckley, which is a delightful concept.

I know how the story will end, but the story itself is what matters.

The pursuit of the story is what matters.

Hinckley will burn. Holmes and Watson will not catch the arsonist. *I want to know the story anyway*, I think as I pass the sign for the fire museum and Hinckley comes and goes. *Tell me the story again.* Years from now, my niece will learn about the Hinckley fire in her sixth-grade social studies class, and I will say, *Do you want to go see? Do you want to walk the place that still bears the scars of this story? What will you understand about this moment in history that you can't from the history book in front of you?*

I wonder what I will tell her about Acadie and what's at stake if I carry on the family silences—and what I perceive as silence—passed down from generations of Babines.

I EXPECT THAT LAKE SUPERIOR WILL BE EXACTLY WHERE I left it a year ago, that lake that feels so ancient and primal and feeds a part of my blood that I can't explain. *Lake Superior never gives up her dead*, as the old adage goes. When I was a kid, we would go past Duluth a bit to Split Rock Lighthouse or Tettegouche State Park but not much farther. I've made a habit of Scamping to Duluth at least once each summer. I know this place, these roads, and that feels important—soon the roads will not be ones I know, and it feels significant that I-35 terminates in Duluth, but that's the point where the journey itself begins, the one that only belongs to me.

Today, as I reach Duluth three hours after the Scamp, the cats, and I leave Minneapolis, we drive past the Aerial Lift Bridge and the historic *William A. Irvin* ore boat anchored and waiting for tourists. The lake is steel blue-gray in the sunshine, pocked with icebergs even in late May as the temperatures climb into the high eighties. Fog hovers between the warmer air and the cold water, but there is no good place to pull off the road and try to photograph it. By the time I find a place to stop, there aren't icebergs anymore, and I'm a little disappointed.

Historians, especially family historians, never give up their dead either.

———

LAKE SUPERIOR NEVER GIVES UP HER DEAD.

It's always a little bit of a shock when I-35 comes to an end and we take the exit right onto Highway 61 that will be London Road through the rest of this part of Duluth, right along the lake with houses that have an unobstructed view of Lake Superior. The road slows to forty miles an hour, then to thirty, and while the traffic behind me would like to go faster, I'm not going to because it's bumpy enough that I'm concerned for the Scamp—and also because I want to peek at those houses, some of which are grand and scream money, others of which are more modest. As I pass the Scandia Cemetery and the iron fencing that marks the Glensheen Historic Estate, I call my mother.

We were there a long time ago, she says, *when the California Grandparents had come to visit after Kim was born in 1983.*

You went to Split Rock, too, I say, *which was always a sore spot, because Kim could always say she'd been there more times than Kristi and me.*

My mother laughs. *That sounds about right. I thought you kids had gone along*, my mother says thoughtfully, but I don't think so. She was still nursing Kim. *I wonder what happened to you and Kristi. Maybe you stayed with Gram and Grandpa?*

I laugh. *Little kids in the car with the California Grandparents for four hours? Yeah, we stayed home.*

The California Grandparents were the kind who ignored the two-hour time difference between Minnesota and California and called deliberately past our bedtimes. It wasn't until decades later that I could reconcile the joyful grins on my grandparents' faces in photographs from our toddlerhood with the chill our relationship acquired—and I came to understand that my grandparents truly did love us, but they had much less interest in their grandchildren when they were no longer small, once we had gained language and reason.

I once said so to my Aunt Teresa, my dad's youngest sibling, and she nodded. *I think you're right. They were good with kids. Not so much when the kids grew up.*

As an adult, I realize this was simply a combination of Silent Generation expectations of adult relationships with kids, or their personalities, or the result of two thousand miles and two time zones. Maybe it just felt jarring because that was not the warm and close relationship we had with my mother's parents, who lived fifteen miles south of us. Like most things, how I understand the relationship is complicated: in my baby book, which is now part of the family archives I continue to gather, there's an entry listing the gift of a Polaroid camera to my parents, with the instruction to "send a picture every week of Karen" and I love the thoughtfulness of the gift, the way it kept them in touch with my parents, considering I was their eldest child's firstborn (and their third grandchild), and by extension, me. Some of my favorite photographs of me were taken with that camera, Polaroids which were returned to us sometime in my twenties as my grandparents were downsizing.

When I was a kid, when we camped on the North Shore, we couldn't afford to tour the glorious Glensheen Historic Estate in Duluth, and we spent our time at Split Rock Lighthouse or Gooseberry Falls, having picnics and hiking and hunting for pretty stones on the shore of the lake. I loved the sound of it, *Glensheen*, the gutteral *G*, the slide of *shhhhh* into the long *ee*. It even sounded expensive, otherworldly. Even now as the Scamp, the cats, and I roll by on the way to Thunder Bay, it's a place that reeks of importance and constantly corrected posture.

As an adult, particularly one who loves history, especially things I have no hope of ever being able to afford, the lure of Glensheen is in what we leave behind and the stories those leavings tell—and the stories they're not allowed to tell. On my very first Scamping trip to Duluth, I made sure Glensheen was in the budget so I could explore those stories for myself. Tour guides were forbidden from

27

discussing the 1977 murder of Elisabeth Congdon and her nurse for many years. If we choose not to tell a story, does that mean it disappears, or does it still live in the space? How does memory linger when all there is is space? If my grandparents never talked about Walt, or the murders, do the stories still exist? Are they still *somewhere*, if I just know how to look for them, if I reconstruct them in documents and archives instead of voices, to hear our history in tidal echoes, in the way that landscape still holds the stories of glaciers and wildfires and earthquakes even if the stories don't exist in living memory of humans? I wanted to think so, so I followed the tour guide and tucked trivia and tidbits into my pockets for later.

On that first visit to Glensheen a few years ago, my tour guide told us that Clara Congdon allowed her daughter to be a tomboy, to shoot guns and ride horses and do unladylike things, but only if she wore a skirt while doing it. The tour began in the stables, which were fancier than any stable had a right to be. I looked down at my own jeans and sturdy Lands' End shoes, my fairly standard Scamping uniform, and inwardly scoffed.

When we walked inside, the tour guide announced, *Given this wealth and the geography of Duluth, it was just as likely that visitors to Glensheen arrived by boat via Lake Superior as they would have by carriage,* and I imagined dark glossy pleasure boats and bright brass fittings, glorious Edwardian fashion with women strapped into S-curve corsets, smartly tailored day wear and glittering evening attire that would not look out of place in New York or London. The walls were paneled in golden wood, the banisters hand carved, the rug wine colored under our feet. When he took us into the reception room, where we would have waited until the Congdon we'd come to see was ready for us, there was nothing to do but stare. I supposed that was the purpose. The Congdons wanted their visitors to be in awe.

Glensheen is its own kind of costume drama, and I love every inch of it, a house and a history separate from real life, something not to be touched, not to be smudged. It's one of those historic estates belonging to men with more money than they knew what to do with, a reminder that at the turn of the twentieth century, thanks to the ore coming out of the Iron Range, Duluth had the most millionaires per capita of anywhere in the United States, and I love that kind of history turned into real life. I wondered what Chester and Clara Congdon's days were like in twenty-two thousand square feet and thirty-nine rooms, among flame mahogany walls and glass fixtures that changed color with natural light or lamplight or the light fixtures of copper in Chester's den made to look like water lilies. At the time, my own apartment was only three hundred square feet. The Scamp was sixty square feet—how many Scamps would fit in the bedrooms?

It was not difficult to place my tall, elegant grandmother Marion in these halls as they joined their own tour group in 1983, my mother probably at the back, with baby Kim strapped to her chest, so as to not bother my grandparents. I imagine my grandmother probably took in the sights with the eye of the interior designer she wanted to become but never did, because when war came, she joined the Cadet Nurse Corps and became a nurse. *Reception rooms*, I thought. *Can you imagine a life in which that's just normal?* I think my grandmother aspired to such things. My grandparents' house in California, with my grandfather's lush rose garden and the burgundy carpet so thick that you could leave footprints in it, had the same kind of rich allure. Even as adults, my sisters and I loved to walk barefoot on that carpet. Had we taken a tour of Glensheen at any point in our childhoods, my mother would have told us *hands in pockets, please.*

Are there any questions? my tour guide asked. I knew he was bracing himself for questions about the murders, and he's not allowed to talk about them. I was hyperaware of the fact that the murders of Elisabeth Congdon and her nurse in 1977 happened only thirteen months after the murders of Walt and Catherine.

Are there any secret passages in the house? I wanted to know, because a girl raised on the Nancy Drew classic *The Hidden Staircase* and Clue is always going to ask. *It would be a shame if there weren't any,* I said.

He looked briefly surprised and said, *I don't know.*

The story the tour guide was not allowed to tell starts like this:

In the 1930s, when Elisabeth Congdon was a single woman in her thirties, she adopted two infant girls, Marjorie and Jennifer. She never married. In 1977, Elisabeth, who had suffered a stroke, was found smothered and her nurse was found beaten to death with a candlestick. Marjorie and her husband Roger were arrested, and the story goes that the motive was nothing more than greed and money, plain and simple. Roger was tried and convicted, but his conviction was later overturned by the Minnesota Supreme Court. In 1983 he confessed to the murders, and he died by suicide five years later.

It's easy to forget that what happened to Elisabeth and her nurse didn't happen outside of time or history. Roger's confession would have been fresh in the news when my parents, baby sister, and California Grandparents visited

Glensheen, and I wonder how my grandparents might have steeled themselves against how close to home this story landed. It's easy to forget that the Glensheen murders were not always historical, the place where it happened not always a museum, their lives and deaths not entertainment for tourists. It's all connected, even if we cannot recognize the ways in a particular moment.

I'm learning what it means to have ethics as the family historian, which silences are necessary, which are not, and what happens when I tell a story that doesn't hurt me individually but has the potential to hurt people I care about. I need to weigh my belief in the need to tell a story against what will happen if I do—or if I don't. Humans might have the right to tell a story, as it may or may not belong to us, but there are consequences in both the telling and not telling. Things We Don't Talk About aren't always unhealthy. Sometimes there's a benefit in not digging too hard into the narrative of a family if that exposure will crack a happy memory and replace it with something painful.

If I believe that stories exist even when there are no conscious memories, then it makes sense to consider where and when and how those stories are preserved, if they're preserved at all. If the stories a family needs to function aren't located in the archives, if they're not carved into the mountains, if they're not in the tales we tell, the memories we share and pass down, if they're no longer embodied or passed down epigenetically, what is left? Is there any benefit in digging up the bones, uncovering all of a family's painful facts, except to understand who they are in the present? If I'm going eastward toward the origin of a family that will end with the deep tragedy that still shades my grandfather's living memory, is that somehow unethical? The rest of that family's history may also live in the body, flashbacks in odd moments triggered by a song, or a smell, or a tone of voice. If we don't tell the stories, will history repeat itself? How much more could we understand about ourselves if we knew the stories of who we were?

My dad says that his parents don't have many stories to tell, which is not exactly true.

They don't even share random stories of their childhood, I say. *They don't launch into anything that begins with "I remember . . ." or "This reminds me of . . ."*

You could always ask them, he says.

That defeats the entire purpose of storytelling, I say. *Besides, they don't talk to us anyway.* They didn't talk to us. They talked near us. Around us. At least that's how I remember it. Very few stories I have from my grandparents were given to me directly. Often they were second- or thirdhand, my dad telling me a story his father had told. I've been trying to accumulate as many of these fragments as I can, filling in the gaps with letters and photographs and military discharge papers to try to construct a more complete story— and sometimes I feel like that's the best work of the family historian, piecing together the story of who we were as new information and documentation becomes available.

Do you want to know the story of what happened that day? my aunt Teresa asked me once.

I nodded. I'd never thought to ask her before, because the story still felt taboo, like it still should not be spoken aloud.

The story my family did not tell—but my aunt would— goes like this: It was May 1976, and my grandparents had owned their house in Novato for three years, the house that would figure in so many of the family memories in the coming decades. My grandfather called his kids, my aunt and uncles, over for a "work party" to help him stain the pergola in the backyard. Teresa would have been fifteen, Uncle Ted would have been twenty-six, Uncle Dennis twenty-four. Uncle Brian and his then fiancée, Joni, were twenty and twenty-one years old and would be married in July, a month after my parents. *Brian and Joni, Ted, Dennis, and I were there*, Aunt Teresa said. *We'd worked hard all day, and we decided that pizza sounded good for dinner, so Ted, Joni, and I went to go get it.*

We walked back in the door with the pizza, all excited and "here's the pizza!" and everybody was just stunned, silent. Then they told us what had happened.

My grandparents went upstairs, leaving the rest of the family downstairs for the rest of the night.

I know now that they were on the phone, making arrangements, but at the time, we were just left to ourselves with the news.

Sometimes the choice not to tell a story, to respect the silences, is the best choice.

LAKE SUPERIOR NEVER GIVES UP HER DEAD.

As I continue north on Highway 61 along the North Shore, I stop to fill the gas tank in Two Harbors and immediately regret trying to make a left turn into the gas station against all the Memorial Day traffic heading back to the Twin Cities. One of the truisms of where I come from is *never turn left without a stoplight between Memorial Day and Labor Day*—and here I am, forgetting everything I've ever been taught about how to literally navigate the world. I *know better*, yet somehow the nerves of the trip are becoming sharper as I forget things I know as I get closer to the Canadian border. I hunch over the steering wheel, every muscle turned to stone, muttering obscenities as I try to figure out how to achieve a full tank of gas to get me into Canada.

Galway judges me silently from his kennel on the passenger seat.

Maeve, who never met an opinion she didn't feel the need to share, snarks at me from the back seat.

Superior never gives up her dead, and it just echoes in my head like a mantra, a thing I know, a strange thing I can trust, and I feel perspective stretch between the microview and the long view, the detail and texture stretching into the clarity of distance. When I take my nephew Henry camping to Duluth when he is ten, the experience will cause me to think differently about focus and scale, particularly about how we come to know things and how we navigate our place in the world. Henry's ADHD gives him a different way of looking at the world, and instead of me trying to impose my view on him, I needed to step into his. While I have great affection for the tiniest of details and can spend hours picking through rocks on the shore, today, Henry's view is much broader. He wants to climb boulders, not look for tiny agates. When I take him to Split Rock Lighthouse, we skip the tour, because he won't have any interest in the discussion of the storms and shipwrecks that led to Congress appropriating the necessary funds to build the light station. What I want to do is put him directly in the path of the lighthouse and watch him light up.

We walk up the steps, ignoring the fog signal house on the left, and we spend a moment looking out at the lake, my nephew tall and slim and blond, his glasses brown rectangles on a face that has to be what my maternal grand-father Kermit looked like as a child. *Are there boats out there? We can't see any.*

The inside of the lighthouse feels cool, white subway tile creating a harsh kind of reflection against the dense black of the narrow cast-iron spiral staircase. Small windows offer light and views as we ascend. Henry looks at the replica third-order Fresnel lens, rotating smoothly on seven quarts of mercury, and I wonder what he is seeing. The Lighthouse Service was absorbed by the Coast Guard in 1939, and my Minnesota grandfather served in light-houses in California before he was commissioned as an of-ficer and transferred to USS *Charlottesville* and sent to the South Pacific during World War II. The lens would have been lit by kerosene, which would have required constant cleaning, and I'm picturing my Minnesota grandfather in this space, *a little fella*, as his fellow sailors called him, who was nimble enough to navigate high and difficult spaces on the ships, and he would have been small enough to climb up and clean the lens. I love the details, the trivia, how each of the lighthouses was constructed to be visually different so they could be identified, how the beacons were also visually unique. I collect details and bits like rocks to store in my pocket, like they are something I can literally carry. I like the microview. I need it. It is how I make sense of the world, but it is not how Henry best makes sense of his world and I appreciate the reminder more than I can articulate.

The young docent from downstairs comes up to wind the cable attached to the weight that makes the lens rotate.

What are you doing? Henry asks, pausing in his pursuit of taking photographs out the windows.

She tells him, *I have to wind this every hour and a half to two hours, and it takes about a hundred and fifty cranks.* He likes this information.

Henry and I go back down the spiral staircase, outside, and are disappointed to see no boats have appeared on the lake in our absence. The night before, the thousand-foot *Presque Isle* had drifted by our campground and we'd gone to watch it navigate into the narrow docks, an experience we both found thrilling. I want to go down to the water and find some of the green quartz that Cora and I had found several years before, but looking for rocks was not something Henry is interested in today, and that reorienting is necessary—this is not my trip, this is his. These are his memories we are making, not just mine.

There are three lighthouse keeper's houses that still stand, each of them identical to each other, because the builders wanted to construct equality between the lighthouse keeper and his assistants. I've been through the house several times before and on previous visits, they've had potatoes and onions cooking in a cast-iron skillet in the kitchen, a smell that always grounds me in home. Gram would take us through a place like this and point out how her family had this and that when she was growing up, but the large view is more important to Henry here—and to me. We walk through the rooms, go upstairs, come down, and as we exit, Henry says, *Can we go back up the lighthouse?*

Sure, I say, *but why?*

Because she just wound it a hundred and fifty times, he says, as if it's obvious.

My legs protest another time up those spiral stairs, but they'll manage.

Absolutely.

He announces to the docent he is back, and up the stairs he goes.

His great-grandfather was in the lighthouse service, I say, letting him go ahead of me.

Wow, she says politely.

Nothing had changed when we reached the top, but that isn't the point.

These days, the beacon at Split Rock Lighthouse is only lit on November 10 to commemorate the sinking of the *Edmund Fitzgerald* in 1975 (and was lit when Gordon Lightfoot died in 2023), but the memory I'm looking for now as I'm heading to Thunder Bay is more complicated. Several years ago, I was sitting in the shade of my Scamp at Burlington Bay Campground in Two Harbors, watching the ore boats headed for the docks at Two Harbors or Duluth and checking the shipping blogs, and I realized that the laker in front of me, rust-red with a narrow diagonal black stripe and thicker white stripe on its bow, was the *Arthur M. Anderson,* the ship that was with the *Edmund Fitzgerald* the night she sank.

Holy shit.

The Anderson *still exists?*

I remember the absolute shock in my bones that the *Anderson* was still in service, because it seemed like it was so far in the past that it should be long gone, tossed for scrap after it had served its usefulness. But then, reality:

1975 was not that long ago.

It was only a year before my parents married, three years before I was born.

That was a surprise, too, somehow, but even the wooden shipwrecks on the floor of Lake Superior are often nearly perfectly preserved, because the environment is not conducive to decay. And yet, in the saltwater Atlantic, the *Titanic* will be gone in a few short decades.

Sometimes I forget that history doesn't always mean gone.

Sometimes I forget that memory lingers in ways we can't articulate.

Sometimes I forget that the past doesn't always mean *beyond our grasp*.

The past and the stories are carried in our bodies in ways we often don't have words for. If we shiver at Dachau, if we feel ill at Ground Zero, if we know what a thunderstorm smells like, we should not dismiss what our bodies know about how to be in the world. The *Arthur M. Anderson*, like Glensheen, is a reminder that history is often compartmentalized, artificially contained, separated from the people that are the stories that history is made of. The *Edmund Fitzgerald* sank in the age of radar, a reminder that it was foolish to trust modern technology so completely and ignore the historical stories of Lake Superior, and timelines of history slide against each other, and it's easy to forget that the grief those families feel is still in present tense.

Days from now, after Lake Superior has long been lost to my rearview mirror, I will find myself in Halifax and wondering at Sable Island, often called the Graveyard of the Atlantic, and I will wonder why we expect this behavior from saltwater and not freshwater. Just because technology has progressed, the lakes aren't any safer than they were a hundred years ago, and if you don't know the history of Lake Superior, if you don't know the sailor's stories of the Witch of November, or the Three Sisters waves, there are consequences.

The lake holds the long view.

CHAPTER THREE

WHEN THE SCAMP, THE CATS, AND I FINALLY ARRIVE in Thunder Bay, six hours after I left Minneapolis, the parking lot of Kakabeka Falls Provincial Park is torn up and full of dust, and the road up to the campground is so rough, so scarred with frost heaves, that I snarl my way up the steep incline toward the campground. I'm out of energy, out of resilience, and the stress of the beginning of a long trip, six hard hours on the road, and a border crossing into another country has caught up with me. My adrenaline rush has long since evaporated. There's always a point on the road where I feel like my brain has been shaken against the sides of my skull for so long that thought is difficult, and it doesn't matter if I'm pulling a camper or not—it's just the bounce and shock of the road, gravity, and those brief moments where the Jeep and I lose contact with the road entirely.

Thunder Bay, Ontario, is a place I have been before, back when we packed three little girls into the back seat of our Blazer, hooked up the pop-up, and set off to camp the circuit around Lake Superior when I was nine, Kristi seven, Kim five. My dad remembers more than I do, how it rained on our way up the North Shore—probably the origin story of my dad's eternal irritation with wet canvas in the pop-up and *don't touch the canvas if it's raining*—and how it was finally nice enough in Thunder Bay that we could dry the sleeping bags and bedding on the clothesline while we went to see Old Fort William. What I don't remember—but my parents do—is the thunderstorm and going back to the camper to find our bedding soaked and then spending the evening in a laundromat drying them out again. Something similar will happen to me in Halifax, days from now, and I will use the campground's Wi-Fi to Skype with my mother to laugh about it.

When we camped when I was a kid, there was a point where we all naturally settled into our particular jobs, and now it all falls to me. There's a lot about the first family camping trip in 1988 that I wish I remembered, how the conversation between my parents started at *let's do this* and how it evolved from there.

Helping Dad level the camper became my job, and I learned well how to interpret the movement of the little bubble on the level, something that felt like a special skill, one that was just mine, one thing that was just between Dad and me. Dad would crank up the roof and pull out the beds, something we eventually took over as we got stronger. I imagine that this was one of those moments of raising girls that he had to consciously work through: just because we were girls didn't mean we couldn't take on the responsibility of important tasks, even ones that required physical strength. It might have been easier and faster for him to do it himself, because he was bigger, but at some point he realized it was okay to delegate. Even if we weren't stronger, we'd have to figure out a way to do it because we couldn't depend on anybody to help us.

It was Kristi's job to pull out the supports for the slide-out bed from where they were stored and with one sister propping up the bed with her back, Kris would slide the pipe into its place on the underside of the bed and the slot on the camper bumper. Then one of us would hop into the camper, climbing over what was still on the floor, and put up the internal supports for the canvas over the beds. Somebody would start rolling out our green World War II–era Army-issue sleeping bags, the ones that Mom had tied a sheet inside to keep them clean, and I liked these sleeping bags better than the newer nylon ones, which tended to slip around on the mattress. These were made of cotton and stayed put much easier. It was Kim's job to transfer our pillows and stuffed animals from the Blazer to the camper. We were only allowed to bring one stuffed animal when we camped, so most of the time we chose our Cabbage Patch Dolls. With the pillows in place, and Erica, Shelly, and Sally propped against them, ready for the next adventure, Mom and Dad usually shooed us away in the direction of the playground, where we could run off our energy. On hot afternoons, that meant the pool or the beach.

As I think back on it, our parents trusting us kids to do tasks, even small ones at a young age, meant more to my own development than I realized at the time: I was capable. We were capable. Our parents thought we were capable. Maybe Dad could have done the jobs easier and faster, but giving us jobs turned us into functional members of the team. That tiny little shift mattered. I've never doubted my own ability to do a thing, to learn a skill, to do something on my own, because my parents never doubted that we could.

WITHOUT MUCH TROUBLE, AND SADLY WITHOUT AN audience other than the cats to be impressed, I back the Scamp into my assigned spot and start the process of setting up camp: leveling, hooking up the electric, filling my collapsible plastic jug with water and setting it on the picnic table, transferring stuff from the Scamp to the Jeep and the Jeep to the Scamp. I open the windows to get some fresh air inside, pull back the curtains for light. The Scamp smells of balsam and mint, the scent of the natural rodent repellent I've used for years, a pleasant smell that has become indelibly ingrained in my brain as *what my camper smells like.*

The Scamp is deeply perfect, partially because it's naturally so and partially because Dad and I have tinkered with it to make it perfect. The white seats of the little front dinette, which Dad and I built five years ago to replace the gaucho couch, store the litter box and the porta-potty. There's a small space under the floor where I've repurposed a thrifted metal basket, which fits as if it was an intentional drawer. I keep my picnic tablecloth, flip-flops, and small secondary jump start battery in there.

Along the driver's side wall, the kitchen: the three-way refrigerator, the propane stove I have never used and will eventually remove entirely, and the sink. One of the first things I did when I bought the Scamp was put a half sheet pan over the top of the stove and secure a microwave to the counter. The long cabinet above the kitchen holds my dishes. I have a sink, covered for counter space. I can hook up to water, but most of the campgrounds I'm in don't have water hookups, so I fill my Brita and keep it on the counter. On this trip, I also packed a SodaStream, which feels a little frivolous for a camping trip, but since I prefer bubbly water to pop, this cuts down on costs and recycling waste.

My bed spans the back wall of the camper, with windows on three sides. It's designed to be the main table for the camper, but I keep it down as a bed permanently. Maybe it doesn't count to go camping with an electric blanket, but this—like it was for my mother in the pop-up—is one of my nonnegotiables, because my body simply does not produce heat. It could be 90 degrees out and if I'm not moving, I'll be cold. I've stuffed extra blankets, towels, and rags into white Ikea pillow covers, and these make great lounging pillows as well as storage. My air conditioning only operates at one power—jet engine—so blankets are necessary. The previous owner of the Scamp bolted a small fan upside down to the cabinets above the bed, a genius idea, and that moves enough air that I often don't need the AC.

In the narrow cabinet over the bed, I store my induction burner, pot, and cast-iron skillet named Agnes, and other things I don't use very often. Everything needs a place, and it needs to stay there, exactly where I expect it to be. Under the bed, Dad and I built a drawer to hold the four cloth bins for my clothes: jeans, tops, unmentionables, and shoes. My inclement weather gear, the rain boots I will be incredibly grateful for when we hit the Maritimes, and my polar vortex–weight parka, are packed in the Jeep.

The closet between the bed and the door over the wheel well is functional support for the roof and it holds my pantry items. Because it's quarter-inch fiberglass, you can't secure anything into it, so Dad and I built a shelving unit out of one-inch schedule 40 PVC, a project that relied on the best of both of us: I had the idea, and he had the technical expertise and tools to manage it. Because the closet creates roof stability (as do the twisted iron supports on the kitchen side), the space itself was a challenge—and it turned out that lightweight PVC was perfect. We created a ladder structure that pressed up against the walls of the closet, with plywood shelves pressing them firm. It's strong, light. The shelves hold my rice, oatmeal, pasta, and kitchen tools. The bottom shelf holds my electric kettle and small Crock-Pot. In later years, I will add a mini Instant Pot and enough spices to rival my stores at home. When I take the niblings—which is the gender neutral term for nieces and nephews—camping, that's where I keep the packets of hot chocolate I offer them for breakfast, because what's the point of being an aunt if you can't make them hot chocolate with marshmallows to go with their oatmeal for breakfast?

I made the muted teal-blue curtains and silver-blue bedspread myself with sewing skills acquired from my mother, which makes the effect of the interior cool in temperature. The white of the fiberglass and cabinets and the cool blue of the bedding and curtains are gentle and soothing, a calming space, one that is good for resetting an overstimulated self. It's a space that *feels good*, especially after a day of driving, when I have no energy or emotional reserves left and I want to pull that rigid skin of the camper over my vulnerable self for protection. Maybe it's glamping to have an electric blanket and pretty curtains, but it seems like those who argue about the purity of what constitutes camping are really, at the crux of it, arguing for misery. Once while camping with the family as adults in Pipestone, Minnesota, I got tired of going back in the camper for more tea, so I pulled out my extension cord, got my electric kettle and big Bredemeijer teapot, and set them up inside the Clam shelter—which led to an existential question among those of us gathered: *how much of glamping is laziness, and how much of it is efficiency?* We decided we didn't care.

———

ONE SUMMER MORNING, AT THE BREAKFAST TABLE WITH my dad, we were watching rain out the patio door, each of us knowing that the work we intended to do on our campers today wasn't going to get done. It was early yet, and we were still on our first pot of tea. It was a lovely, slow morning.

When you went camping when you were a kid, where did you go?

He thought for a minute, and it was as if I could watch his mind stand up in Minneapolis and wing back over decades and miles to his Southern California childhood, before he said, *I remember going to Sequoia and Kings Canyon and camping in the Lodgepole Campground.* I laughed at the specificity he still held after more than sixty years. My mother had camped with her parents in a small pop-up, and I wished I'd asked her more about it before she died.

He continued, in that voice reserved for old memories. *Dad had gotten a huge canvas tent, and it was so big we called it the Taj Mahal. We had a couple of old army cots, the kind with the wooden supports, so we could have slept on those—I don't remember.*

There's a photograph somewhere, somewhere I can't find, of a big tent on a beach and my grandparents, with a toddler that I imagine is my father. *When did you start camping?*

He paused. *I'm not sure,* he said, and I could almost see him flipping through photographs in his mind like a Rolodex, trying to place the right memory in the right place at the right time. *Probably when I was about seven or eight?*

My dad would have been seven or eight in the late 1950s, and *that would have made Uncle Dennis and Uncle Brian really little*, I said. My dad and his brothers were nearly perfectly stair-stepped boomer kids—Dad in 1949, Ted in 1950, Dennis in 1952, Brian in 1955. Teresa came along in 1961. I wondered if Uncle Brian stayed with his grandparents until he was old enough to join them on their camping trips.

He nodded, and whatever he was remembering, whatever stories he was putting to that particular geography, he couldn't quite put into words.

That's about the same age we were when you and Mom decided you wanted to go camping with us, I said. *It's hard to imagine your mother sleeping on the ground, but sometimes I forget they were young and energetic once, wanting to make the same kind of memories with their kids that you and Mom did later.* That evolved as I bought my own camper and the niblings came along, that in addition to me taking each kid camping with me separately, sometimes my parents would pack up their camper, I'd pack up mine, we'd grab a kid or two, and make ourselves a multi-generational trip, even if it was just to a park ten miles away.

Dad sipped his tea. *Dad had a small utility trailer with three-foot sides, and he'd built a box with rope handles that slid perfectly into the trailer, and that held all our cooking stuff.* Of course he built a box that fit his trailer perfectly—this is my grandfather. Of course he did. We often joked that Grandpa traded in his motor home for a new one when he ran out of things to tinker with. Tinkering is both a desire and skill set, I decided. If what you want doesn't exist, make it. *We had a nesting set of pots and pans that had plates that fit on the top of the stack, and it might have been made out of cast aluminum, but it might not have been aluminum, since it was the '50s*, he said.

I imagine there was a lot of army surplus they probably picked up.

Probably.

Grandpa probably had a lot of war-oriented camping experience, I said, and I was envisioning my grandfather having learned the hard way how to build a fire in less-than-ideal circumstances while sleeping on the cold ground in Europe, how to create shelter, and even though he'd been a Boy Scout, I imagine that training only went so far.

That's a specific kind of knowledge, my dad agreed.

When I start to question the relationship with my grandparents, who had enthusiastically loved us when we were little and then, very quickly it seemed, wanted little to do with us, I instead focus on how we—as a family of Minnesota Babines—deliberately worked to construct the relationship between parents and children and grandchildren in a much different way. It wouldn't happen by accident. It would happen in the way, at Frontenac State Park, my dad handed five-year-old Henry a ball-peen hammer to pound a piece of firewood into the Kindling Cracker, a cast-iron wedge surrounded by a circular frame, so that you place your wood on the wedge, smack it with a hammer or small sledge, and it cracks your wood into smaller pieces without putting your fingers at risk.

Dad sat on the picnic table bench, holding the wood in place with gloved hands. My mother and I supervised from our chairs.

You keep going until I tell you to stop, Dad said.

Henry held the hammer with both hands and smacked the wood, then looked up at his Boppa, and promptly lost his hand-eye coordination.

No, that's my hand, Dad quipped.

Sorry, Henry said sheepishly and managed to make contact with the wood again.

Doing good, Henry, I said, and I was remembering how my sisters and I learned to build fires on our trips when we were kids.

You're doing super, Dad said, noting Henry hadn't made much progress. *Want me to hit it again?*

Yeah, Henry said, and Dad tapped it with his own hammer, splitting it a little more.

Henry crouched on the ground. *Look, it's going up!* he said, looking at the split in the wood.

If you hit it a few more times, it'll split! Dad said, and Henry focused on the wood, pounding with his little hammer, and the wood split neatly into two. Henry's grin was like sunshine in its joy.

I still remember the first time we took Cora to the RV show at the Minneapolis Convention Center the week before her first birthday. Thousands of square feet of every kind of camper imaginable, from tiny teardrops to million-dollar Class A motor homes with marble countertops, steam showers, and washers and dryers neatly tucked away in cedar-lined closets. Cora wore a long-sleeved white shirt layered under a maroon tee bearing the mascot of my alma mater, jeans, and brown shoes with white socks. I looked at her and decided there isn't much that's cuter than babies in jeans. She had wispies of finely spun blonde cotton candy hair; her blue eyes were bright. I'd been dreaming about taking her camping with me since long before she was born. When Dad and I pulled the front couch out of the Scamp to replace it with a two-person dinette that could fold back down to a bed, it was with her—and her brothers who did not yet exist—in mind.

We wandered the aisles of dreams on wheels, the toy haulers, the travel trailers with honest-to-goodness porches on them, the shiny park models that made me wonder if I could live in a tiny house. We debated floor plans, the relative merits of outdoor kitchens, the ridiculousness of campers with fake fireplaces. My dad and I, carrying the Babine Tinkering Gene, gathered small space ideas from these new models to incorporate into our own campers. We mocked the expensive Class As under our breath and wondered *at what point can you not call that camping anymore?* We got deeply philosophical about it over our ice cream.

Can you call it camping if you don't sleep on the ground?

Is it camping if you have an electric blanket? A microwave? A fridge?

We waffled on those questions but drew the line on the cedar-lined closet.

My mother simply humored us.

Here's the moment that matters, the reason I love this story:

We carried Cora for most of our wanderings, but she eventually protested. She wanted to practice stair climbing and going back down the stairs on her belly, bump-bump-bump, like my mother, her Nana, had taught her. She wanted to walk, so we let her, following as she toddled her tiny jeans-wearing butt down the green carpeting meant to remind us of spring grass rather than February gloom. She was uneven enough on her feet to make us nervous, but we picked her up when she fell, and she got back to her feet and kept moving at the speed of cheerful baby.

Then I noticed an odd phenomenon:

As she wobbled by, all the grandpa-aged men instinctively moved between Cora and the camper hitches, so that if she fell, she wouldn't crash into the hitch. I watched, fascinated, as this happened again and again—some men would be deep in conversation as we passed, and without thinking, they angled their bodies to protect her, as if they were all just aware of a tiny, vulnerable person. Over and over this happened, just that small shift of the body, as if the instinct was passed from one grandfather to the next, and I was reminded how grateful I am that Cora has my dad for a grandpa.

Maybe this change in family dynamic was simply a necessary generational change, but that seems too simplistic. In the context of my dad's parents and the California Babines, it felt like the stability of a meaningful adult life meant doing what you're supposed to do to contribute to society. You get married, you have kids. It's *just what adults do*, the expectation, what's normal, and even as Gen X started to question traditional modes of being, it was the Millennials who were able to put a lot of that into action—only to be blamed for the decline of marriage, the decline of home ownership and the dinner party, the baby bust, and a thousand other things that my grandparents valued to regain some semblance of stability after the war, my parents' generation often begrudgingly tolerated, and future generations will reject, because that's not how we best construct our relationships. I don't know that my grandparents had any idea what to do with a grandchild with advanced degrees and a well-used passport instead of—and not in addition to—a husband and kids. I suspect it confused them greatly.

And I said so to my dad, as he stood outside one of the Scamps at the factory in Backus on that exploratory trip in 2008. My father agreed, leaned in the door of a thirteen-foot Scamp, and promptly hit his head on the ceiling. He is six-five. This happens. I stood inside, straightened my spine to my full five-eight height, and barely brushed the rat fur—it's marine headliner fabric, but everyone calls it rat fur—on the ceiling, and I realized I would hit my head on the air conditioner, so I'd have to be careful. This particular model was the standard, with the small couch against the front window that could turn into bunk beds. The other thirteen-foot model had a bathroom where the couch was. I toed off my shoes and laid down on the bed and just barely fit, but I'm mostly a side sleeper, so I could make it work.

What about a bathroom? my dad asked. *They make them with bathrooms. You might want that in the middle of the night.*

I didn't want a bathroom—I wanted the full camping experience of cooking outside, using campground bathrooms, meeting people. I had memories of my mother packing the three of us off to the bathroom and the unique camaraderie of chance conversations with strangers.

You might change your mind as you get older, he said. *At my age, it's something I really appreciate.*

Maybe, I said, *but I think I'll cross that bridge when I get to it.*

You might really like the extra space in the sixteen-foot, he commented later. *Especially if you ever get the dog you keep talking about.*

I nodded. Camping with cats would be an adventure. While camping with dogs is not unusual, I'm not sure if I knew anybody who camped with cats. If I was planning to be on the road for weeks at a time, I might as well bring them. They'd hate it, of course, but they'd hate boarding more. Galway had a history of abuse and abandonment before I adopted him, so leaving him was not really an option. I'm not sure if I even knew cat harnesses and cat leashes existed. Even if I did, Galway and Maeve would not have consented.

We toured some sixteen-footers, and I filed away his advice, weighing it against what I really wanted, and what I really wanted was the thirteen-foot. I had never wanted a stick-built camper, never wanted a teardrop, never wanted a Class B campervan, and I never really seriously considered the sixteen-foot. I'd wanted *this camper* for a long time. Two months later I found what I wanted for sale online, two hours away in Cleveland, and I bought it on the spot, much the same way my parents had the pop-up, because I knew the moment was right.

━━

WHEN EVERYTHING IS SET UP, THE CATS COME OUT OF their kennels and the kennels go back into the Jeep. Neither is an outdoor cat and Galway is scared of everything, so his primary goal is a place to hide. Maeve likes to sit on the front dinette and yell at wildlife, so the boundaries of the camper are for their safety and hers. More than one veterinarian has commented that she has the vocabulary of a sailor.

As I finish my outside campsite chores, putting down the stabilizer jacks, setting out my zero-gravity chair and small table, I become grateful that I packed leftovers for dinner. I am too tired to contemplate chopping potatoes, onions, and carrots to cook in aluminum foil over a fire that will take at least an hour to burn down to coals. There's so much stress and energy involved in getting on the road that you really do need more than one night to settle into the rhythm of camping, of the road, of disconnecting yourself from a life where the scenery out your front window doesn't change on a daily basis. You have to give your physical body a chance to catch up with your mental body, so after everything is set up,

I go for a walk. The campground is pretty empty, so it's quiet and lovely. If it were later in the day, we'd call it the Evening Walkabout, a stretch of time after dinner in which it's become ritual for campers to walk their dogs, stretch their legs, and take stock of who else is in the campground.

———

MY GRANDFATHER ONCE TOLD ME THE CHILDHOOD STORY of his family driving from California to Kennebunk, Maine, in 1930 in the family's 1929 Model A sedan when my great-great-grandfather Joseph was stricken with a stroke. My great-grandfather, Bill Sr., had been born in Nova Scotia, but his parents and siblings had been living in Maine for decades. It was one of the few times my grandfather told me a story about his childhood when I asked, rather than me hearing a story secondhand, the way most stories came down to me. He recalled that most of the trip was filled with flat tires, rain, and mud. In an email, he wrote:

> We got up every morning at 5:00 a.m. and Mother fixed breakfast. Then we loaded up the car and Dad drove until 9:00 p.m., stopping only for gas and to change flat tires. During that trip, our parents would stop and check out the motor courts for cleanliness, and if it was okay, we would stay the night. If not, they would continue until they could get one that was clean. While they were checking out the motel, Walt and I got out of the car and went to the bathroom, but when we came out, THEY WERE GONE. The proprietor took us under her wing and tried to comfort us, but to no avail. Two six-year-old boys in strange Kansas, and we didn't know where our parents were. Mother and Dad discovered

us missing at the next stop when they told us to get out and NO BOYS. Dad drove back and got us—and as I remember it was about an hour, and were we relieved to see him.

I wonder what it took to keep two small boys so quiet that their parents didn't even notice they weren't in the car. My grandfather told this as an amusing story, and maybe it's not my place either as a granddaughter or family historian to suggest this is a truly heartbreaking story, that *something* turned those small boys so invisible that their parents did not realize they were not there. I have a black-and-white photo of my grandfather and Walt dressed in sailor suits with their mother Catherine, sitting at a picnic table eating lunch. A Model A is in the background, and I assume Bill Sr. is taking the photograph. The boys look about the right age, so it's possible that they took this photograph on that trip. A single memory often means little—they only make meaning in the accumulation.

When we were little, the same age he was on that trip to Maine, he was the grandpa who would tell us, *Eat it, it'll put hair on your chest!* only to have us wail in horror, *But Grandpa, I don't want hair on my chest!* There was a period of time when he called all of us granddaughters George with a twinkle in his eye just to watch us protest with all the indignance of small children, *My name's not George!* Of his thirteen grandchildren, eleven of us were girls, and there was a mischievous part of my grandfather that liked to see if he could rile us up. That kind of relationship—and its sense of humor—largely stopped by the time I was six or seven. It happened so suddenly that I had no idea what caused it, if there was something I did, or we did, and I couldn't figure out what that could be.

Later, I'd think about that kind of emotional bruising when I discovered a treasure trove of draft cards on Ancestry .com, which included all four of my great-grandfathers' World War I draft cards, and both my grandfathers' World War II draft cards. Draft registrations, like many official documents, are unusual ways of documenting information that feel more textured than simply *old-fashioned*. My maternal great-grandfather Ulfert Kleene, asked to describe himself as tall/medium/short, wrote *tall* in perfect Palmer Method penmanship, and when asked if he was slender/medium/stout, wrote *slender*. These weren't the questions Bill Sr. typed on his World War II draft card, which listed his address as *2 miles west of Ramona, California*, and listed his employer as *myself*. At the top, in pencil, written by an unknown hand, it reads *10-22-42 Kennebunk, Maine*; since they were in California then, I asked my dad about it.

I don't know, he said, sitting at the kitchen table, holding the printout of the draft card. *We could call and ask.*

Okay, I said, and Dad dialed Grandpa, turned on speakerphone, and set the phone on the table between us.

I told Grandpa that I'd found his and Walt's draft cards—and that I'd found his dad's too.

Dad wasn't drafted, he said.

My grandfather did not like to be contradicted and especially not by children, no matter that I was past thirty, but I traded raised eyebrows with my dad.

I've got his draft card right here, I said.

No, he said. *He wasn't drafted.*

And that was the end of it. I wanted to ask about the October 1942 date, or why it had Kennebunk, Maine, next to it, but there was no more conversation to be had. I wanted my grandfather to be excited or at least pleased by what I'd found, that this draft card and my interest in his history and his family might somehow restore our relationship. Instead I listened to him tell me I was wrong.

I wasn't wrong. Dad shrugged when I gave a silent, exaggerated sigh from across the table, and I let Dad move through the concluding pleasantries. He hung up the phone and we just looked at each other for a long moment. It wasn't until years later that I wondered if my grandfather simply found it too painful to talk about his dad at all, under any circumstance. I wondered if he'd had a visceral reaction to the question, an overwhelming wave of grief, even decades after his father's death, and the silence and silencing was simply a defense mechanism. Maybe it had nothing to do with me at all. But it still stung.

It made me think about how families are constructed and the work the Minnesota Babines have done to create something different than how my dad's family worked. My dad grins now when he says that he can't imagine talking to his parents like the three of us talk to him. In the last few years, my sisters and I have started flipping Dad the bird when he deserves it, which we all now refer to as a *disrespectful display of affection*. It makes him howl with laughter. Once, Dad said something that required both middle fingers and he laughed, said that *I can't imagine flipping off my dad*. I couldn't either. It's true that he didn't have that kind of relationship with his dad that he has with the three of us, but I suspect that my grandfather had very specific ideas of filial respect, and part of that meant keeping strict lines between the generations. He would always be the father, my dad would always be the child, the three of us would always be the grandchildren.

We're lucky that at some point my parents and the three of us decided that we liked each other as people, and our parents have grown to see us as equals in many ways, even though I don't think it was ever a conscious decision on their part. The truth is that my parents raised three girls who became very strong, very strong-willed people, though the growing pains of this relationship adjustment took some effort in our twenties. Dad will often talk about 2005 as a turning point, a moment somewhere in Montana or North Dakota, where somebody snaps a photograph of Kristi, crouched on the muddy ground, bright yellow DeWalt drill in her hands, bright orange carrot stuck between her back teeth like a cigar. Kristi's putting down the scissor jacks on my parents' travel trailer with the drill so she doesn't have to crank it by hand. We're in the midst of something we haven't done since I graduated from high school: a family camping trip. I was twenty-six, Kristi twenty-four, Kim twenty-two and just graduated from college, and in hindsight, maybe that's odd, single adult children voluntarily going camping with their parents, but it wasn't weird for us. What's not in the photograph is how we talked politics on those miles, particularly marriage equality, and Dad says something we've never heard before: "You might be right." It's the first time he's said so out loud, acknowledging changing political views, particularly ones that are rooted in religion and religious morality, the first time he's even hinted that his children might hold views that are more right than his. Because in his world, his parents were infallible, not because they were but because they wanted to be. It's the first time he'd considered the shifting construction of family, that the building of relationships doesn't happen by accident, or by expectation or fiat, and we've considered how much children contribute to that construction.

I always had a traditional kind of respect for my parents, he said later.

Had? Or was it required of you?

He thought for a minute. *Maybe it was required.*

There was a clear hierarchy in the California Babine house, and Bill and Marion were at the top. They valued obedience and respect and viewed any disagreement or questioning or discussion as *dis*obedience, *dis*respect. There was no discussion, no alternate ideas or ways of doing things. There was only one right way to do things, and that was their way, and it was to be done immediately, without question. Sometimes I wonder about that vertical construction of family relationships, and I wonder if that traditional kind of elder respect, as my grandparents demanded, is rooted in infallibility, in clear standards of right and wrong. My grandparents were never wrong, as I remembered in the conversation with my grandfather about his father's draft card. I wonder if vertical relationships can function without those in power wielding infallibility.

And I said so to my dad once: *I suspect not.*

I had the same kind of respect for Kermit and Phyllis, my dad said.

Did you? Did you feel they demanded the same kind of respect from you—or was it earned?

Dad paused. *It was earned.*

My father would say that he lucked out in the in-law sweepstakes. In the relationships that my dad married into, there was no tearing down, because there was no vertical axis. There was only the horizontal, the foundation, the grounding in who we were because of where we were.

As I CONTINUE MY STROLL AROUND THE CAMPGROUND, IT'S easy to think of this kind of deliberate construction of identity. Like all campgrounds, the Whispering Hills is aspirational. It's like all the other provincial parks of my experience, each campsite private and lined by three sides of trees, but the names of the campers around me offer some clues as to who we want to be on the road, like character traits, which includes my parents' Excel. Freedom. Apex. Enlighten.

Predators that suggest dominance: Eagle. Cougar. Raptor. White Hawk. Arctic Wolf.

Destinations that suggest rugged individualism: Denali. Open Range. Montana. Heartland Pioneer.

Smaller campers get cute names: Feather, Mini Winnie, Hummingbird.

Scamp.

There's something weirdly—and uncomfortably—American about such things.

I'd love to give my Scamp a cutesy name, like Shrimp Scampi, or Dumpling, but nothing's ever stuck. It's interesting that whenever the question is asked *what did you name your Scamp?* either in Facebook groups or on fiberglass RV forums, they're almost all gendered female, many named after mothers or grandmothers, or other strong women in the camper's life. I once woke from a dream in which my camper's name was Haiku, the tiniest of poetries, and the name bold and black under the back window, and I even had a quote from Bashō under the porch light next to the door. Maybe "The dragonfly tries, / try as it might, but can't land / on that blade of grass" or "With every gust, / the butterfly changes place / on the willow tree." Bashō's is the poetry of movement, and as I've been driving north with him in mind, his *Narrow Road to the Deep North*—or in another translation, *Narrow Road to the Interior*—the linguistic loveliness of north and interiority feels potent, because it's without distraction.

———

ANOTHER PLACE, ANOTHER TIME: THE JAPANESE HAVE JUST bombed Pearl Harbor and Bill Sr. and Catherine's Southern California world, so close to the base at Coronado, has become instantly on edge. I would like to think that my grandfather and Walt would have been part of these conversations, concerns about what's next, wondering about a draft, but the boys are still teenagers, and I wonder at what point Bill Sr. considers his sons men. Each family constructs the relationship it wants with itself, though as I consider all the fragments of data and story I have, it's worth remembering that sometimes that relationship is out of everybody's control, whether the factors are internal or external. I wonder if my grandfather's kitchen table was the place where he learned that his own children should be seen and not heard. Dad said once that his childhood dinner table was for eating, not talking, something that he changed when the three of us arrived, our dinner table each night filled with stories of the day.

Then draft papers come for Bill Sr. He's drafted in the fourth draft, the Old Man's Draft. I imagine Bill sitting at the kitchen table in Ramona, holding his draft card, not saying anything. He's not sober, but I imagine he hasn't been sober for a long time. He is fifty-two. Catherine is fifty-one. He's given up working as a glazier after he lost his job in Bakersfield in 1938 and they moved to Ramona. He's been a house painter ever since, and he's good at that, too, meticulous about cleaning his brushes, and if the alcohol affects the straightness of his lines, it can be fixed. Houses don't usually need straight lines. He wouldn't have had language for PTSD or any of the effects of war he self-medicated with alcohol, but with distance and decades of mental health advancement, that's how I interpret how he came to be who he was, how he made the decisions he did. I couldn't find statistics for how many veterans of World War I were called up in the Old Man's Draft.

He knows that when the boys turn eighteen in October 1942 and graduate from high school in 1943, they will face the war. One son will go into the Army in Europe; the other will follow the Marines into the South Pacific, but he doesn't know that yet. The boys will be separated, because Walt's eyesight is better than his brother's, and the Marines are taking the best of the best. I wonder if my great-grandfather voices his fears to anyone or if he simply takes his comfort from the bottle, the only place that the shelling and the mustard gas and the cries and the pounding of gunfire from thirty years ago are quiet. I imagine he holds that draft card in a much different grip than he held his first draft card in 1917.

On July 28, 1943, a few weeks after the boys leave for boot camp, my great-grandfather took a shotgun out to the back shed. That's always the phrasing: *he took a shotgun out to the back shed.* He was not going back. The *Escondido Times-Advocate* reported the death in the newspaper, with the deputy coroner ruling the death self-inflicted and observing that "Babine had been despondent." What reads most tragic to me is that the Fourth Draft was to take stock and register the older men for service on the home front, but when I told Dad about this, he wondered, *Did he misunderstand the draft? That he wouldn't get shipped overseas?* And that's what I assume,

that whatever depression or PTSD or other mental illness
he might have had simply overpowered him when he was
drafted. Maybe it was exacerbated by the knowledge that his
sons would be sent into battle. I don't know what he might
have faced in those awful days, the human brain trying to
cope with what horrors humans do to each other in the name
of power and expect them to forget what they've seen when
they come home. I'm remembering all the episodes of the
radio show *The Shadow* that I've listened to over the years,
but in particular I remember the end of "The Silent Avenger,"
which aired in 1938 and tells the story of Danny Bricker, the
brother of an inmate on death row, convinced by his brother
to take revenge on all the people who put him in the electric
chair. Danny is shell-shocked after his service in World War
I, and in the story I hear the echoes of Bill Sr. and Walt. At
the end, The Shadow says,

> *There is no credit. No glory in the death of Danny Bricker,*
> *Commissioner Weston. He was a victim, a human instru-*
> *ment of destruction, fashioned by mankind, that teaches men*
> *to kill their enemies in time of war, yet expects them to forget*
> *their murderous art in time of peace. Danny Bricker was an*
> *enemy of society—a killer. But only because you and I and*
> *countless thousands made him one.*

When Grandpa and Walt came home for the funeral,
the sheriff asked if they wanted the shotgun back. They said
no. Bill Sr.'s death certificate reads *accident* so he could be
buried in consecrated ground, the rosary recited the evening before his funeral mass. He would be buried in St.
Mary's Cemetery.

I want to know what other little falsehoods lie in the records I have at my fingertips, in my archives and databases, what it feels like to stand in the presence of the ones that recognize human suffering and do their best to alleviate it for the living, figure out their place in the world and how to navigate it.

I am aware of the gravity of this Scamping journey toward Acadie and the tangible reminder that the Babines existed, that their story matters, that all those fragments are not lost to history. Seems obvious to read Longfellow on the road to Acadie, wondering what place-names I would still find, what the happy valley might feel like under my feet:

> And away to the northward
> Blomidon rose, and the forests old, and aloft on the mountains
> Sea-fogs pitched their tents, and mists from the mighty Atlantic
> Looked on the happy valley, but ne'er from their station
>   descended.

On the road to Acadie, I wonder if there is any story at all, or only fragments that allude—or elude, even—to how the Babines became who we are, and I wonder if there's no deeper meaning to be found on this road except the accumulation of those fragments that become different stories, depending on how they're arranged.

CHAPTER FOUR

THIS FIRST MORNING AT KAKABEKA FALLS, IT'S A morning for coming awake slowly, watching the sun through the Scamp curtains changing the blue as the angle intensifies. I like to have the windows cracked overnight so that the morning usually begins with crisp air even before I'm aware of it. I haven't had a morning like this in a while, and I'm a person who loves morning, loves to brew a pot of tea and watch the world come to itself, an inch at a time, the evolution of thin sun snagging on the underside of clouds, first the barest of peach, then salmon, then the most shocking of pinks, before it eases itself into the fullness of being. You can't rush a sunrise, even the most pedestrian of them, the ones you watch sitting at the kitchen table or the dinette of your camper with cats who think they should have been fed hours ago. It's a good lesson on this first morning of the trip, just to slow down. Maeve and I have different ideas about the definition of "early" and "sleep in," as she bullied me into getting up and feeding her. The earplugs worked for a while, but I finally gave up. Galway usually sleeps with me, at the foot of the bed, usually under whatever covers he can find; Maeve's favorite place is in her bed on the front dinette.

On the days you're on the road, there's a part of the brain that clicks into place: you wake up, and you're pointed out, away, already calculating what needs to be done to get back on the road. Even on slow mornings, I have to fight against the urge to hurry. The morning—even if it's not great weather—exists for itself. It's good to be reminded of that.

The campsites here are private, surrounded by trees, and there's something elementally satisfying about that, almost a reorienting of the senses, a reminder that sight is often the least effective way to know anything about the world. It's quiet here, which is not the same as silent. Across the campground, I can hear children yelling and the dog I heard last night. I slept better than I expected to, and I'm slowly coming to terms with disconnecting from technology, the ability to have everything I want to know at my fingers, and relying on what I know in my body. I'm used to checking the weather first thing in the morning, and that's not an option now and won't be for the next month because my phone won't work in Canada.

So, I will listen.

I can feel the layers of personality I have worked so hard to construct start to fall away, dissolving into the quiet of the wind in the trees, and it feels like I'm regaining that person I am when I camp, without all the filters. The social aspect of solo camping holds little appeal—camping alone together—because the point of being alone means that I don't have to carry any of my personalities with me. A weekend where I'd always have to be on, performing a particular character with people I'd likely never see again, sounded terrible. There are Scamp rallies all over the country, great gatherings of people with campers like mine who share so many of the same interests and experiences.

After my friend Marya buys a Scamp a few years ago, I will text, *want to go to the Scamp Homecoming next year and be antisocial?*

And she'll text back, *YES!*

Whenever I'm with people, I'm always on—which is why I like the brief chats as people pass by my campsite. Being on doesn't last very long, and then I can turn it off. Maybe this all feels easy—and inevitable—now, but being solo with the Scamp was not always so, particularly on that first trip out of my Ohio driveway back in 2008, when I started to understand that there were layers to being solo, that it's more than just being alone, on a social level, but also mechanically and logistically. Maybe the mechanical lesson had to come first.

It seems simple enough, I thought, standing there in my driveway, looking from the Jeep to the Scamp and back to the Jeep. *Just hook the thing up. Hitch, meet stinger.*

Spoiler: it was not that simple.

It was one thing to hitch the Jeep to the Scamp with somebody to help, another thing entirely to do it on my own. But there wasn't an alternative, so I might as well get to it.

It took an hour and a half to get out of the driveway.

I made sure that the tongue was cranked high enough so that I could get the hitch ball under it, and then I made my first attempt at backing it up. I was somewhere in the ballpark, maybe a couple inches off, so I pulled ahead and tried again. Didn't get close enough. Tried to back up just a little, but not close enough. Pulled ahead, tried again. Off by just a little. Pulled ahead, tried again.

I learned a very valuable lesson here—*you cannot negotiate with inches*. If you're not close enough to hitch the thing, pull ahead and start from scratch. I hoped none of my neighbors were watching, because this was embarrassing.

After about forty-five minutes, *success!* I got the hitch ball underneath the hitch and I reached for the crank on the jack to lower it—

—and the handle wouldn't go around because it was catching on the Jeep's spare tire.

I was confused. *We did this fine a few weeks before when I'd bought the Scamp, so what's the problem now?* No idea.

I stood there for a minute, weighed my options, and then decided to try to come in at an angle, and after six or eight more embarrassing attempts I managed to get the hitch ball near the hitch, then the jack handle worked— but then the hitch wouldn't go on the ball. Just straight up refused.

I stared at it for a few minutes. Sometimes I'm a good problem solver, and sometimes I'm not. My dad was out of reach and of no help to me, so I was on my own if I actually wanted to get out of my driveway and go camping.

Eventually, I figured out how to finesse the little lever on the hitch, and like magic, suddenly I was actually hooked up. The lever was down, and I snapped the padlock on it before it changed its mind.

Then the back stabilizer jacks decided to cause problems. They're not leveling jacks—they're simply there for stability. I got the right one up without much of a problem, the same kind of jacks I'd learned on with the pop-up, which retract to be stored parallel to the back bumper. The left one had other ideas, and no amount of WD-40, curses, or bloody knuckles would convince it to budge. By this time, I got some Dad advice, and he suggested taking it to the gas station / mechanic around the corner to see if they could help. It was a good idea as any, so I said goodbye to the cats, locked the front door, and with extreme care, put the Jeep in drive.

And half-intentionally broke off the jack as I pulled out of the driveway.

I didn't do it completely on purpose, but I figured it would happen, and there wasn't anything I could do about it. The guy at the gas station understood rusty bolts and used his fancy impact wrench to take it off, and he didn't charge me for it. It was a moment where I realized that not only did I have to do everything myself, I *had* to, because there was always the stigma of *if you want to do it by yourself, then do it*. Asking for any help not only negated my sense of self as a solo woman camper but also dropped a sticky film of *of course you need help, you're a woman, and you're by yourself*. So I learned a lot the hard way, and then I learned the nuances that largely added up to *I don't want help*, but that's an oversimplification.

It's not that it's not nice for somebody to notice that you're alone and to offer to help you back up, or some other task of towing that isn't easy to do by yourself. Of course it is, and when I was starting out, I would have welcomed it. If somebody looks like they're having trouble starting their fire, I might go over and offer a fire starter if it wouldn't embarrass them. But the reality is that I camp alone. I tow alone. And while men often ask women if they want help backing up their camper, nobody asks my dad if he wants help. And often, it's not "do you want help backing it in?"—it's usually "do you want me to back it in for you?" I've started calling this the Benevolent Sexism of the Road, and these days it annoys me. A few weeks from now, in Digby, Nova Scotia, I will encounter a truly spectacular version:

The man behind my camper is likely married to the woman who checked me in at the office a few minutes ago, and as I drive toward my site, he comes tootling down the path to where I'm backing in. He's probably in his late sixties, short, portly, and has a kind face. I imagine he's a wonderful grandfather. I can't figure out immediately what he's doing or why he's getting in my way, so I just wait as he walks behind me into the campsite. He sets himself up to help me back in. It's a nice gesture, but he's in my way, which is dangerous. I'm really, really good at backing up the Scamp. I've been doing it for six years. Once, I took the Scamp to the factory for repairs, and I backed it into their garage smooth as silk, on the first try. I didn't even have to pull it forward to straighten it out. I felt like my entire gender was at stake, felt the weight of countless women camping alone on my shoulders, and I didn't want to give anybody the ammunition that I'd fail to do this because I'm female. I got out of the Jeep and handed the keys to the guy, and he said, slowly, with deep respect, "We get guys in here, forty, fifty, sixty years old, who can't back in as well as you." I just grinned.

Back to the portly man with the kind face: it's going to hurt the dude's feelings if I say something snarky, and I have an overdeveloped sense of Minnesotan Lutheran guilt, so I let him stand there and wave me back. It's no skin off my nose to ignore him. He's not actually helping me. He's in my way. But at least I can see if I'm going to run him over.

When I'm mostly where I want to be on the pad, I hop out to check the general levelness of things, and I need to put a block under the left wheel, so I pull on my leather gloves and get to work. The state of my gloves, which are stained with oil and dirt—and probably some blood, because I am a tissue-skinned Babine—should be a good indicator that I know what I'm doing. I get back in the Jeep and slowly back over the block, then hop back out to check whether it's level enough. I subscribe to the *close enough* standard of level. I actually prefer the Scamp not to be exactly level, just a little higher on the driver's side, where the head of my bed is, because I don't like sleeping downhill. I always have the hitch a little higher than the back end. It has to be close to level if I want the fridge to work.

When I'm satisfied with the general set up, the man ambles around the side of the Scamp and says to me, not unkindly, "Before long, you'll be able to do this with your eyes closed!" I smile tightly, because I know he didn't mean anything insulting by it. Now that I've been doing this for years by myself, I could do it with my eyes closed—but it bothers me, because well-intentioned or not, it's still sexist and it's still damaging and it still pisses me off.

The social layers of camping solo came more slowly, somehow. Once I was Scamping outside of St. Louis when the morning started to heat around me in a way that felt dangerous, and I hung my pretty shade curtains on the sides of my awning in that heavy morning sunshine, so thick with humidity, so I could enjoy my morning tea more fully. The only times I prefer to be inside my camper are when it's raining—otherwise, it's like a little tent on wheels with a door I can lock. The air pressure was starting to become oppressive, though, and it wasn't even 8:00 a.m. yet. This felt like it was going to be a wild day, though I couldn't have predicted two storms so severe that I barely had time to take down the awning, throw the cats in their kennels, and drive down to the shower house for shelter.

The morning was quiet and dense and full of warning and still around me as I drank my tea, not even in a mood to read or write in my Scamp journal, too tired to do much but drink my very strong Assam and hope it would reach into my brain and threaten it awake. I've determined that camping with cats is like having kids, and I, of course, don't want kids. They don't go to sleep when you tell them, and they're fighting before the sun is up. I think the actual fighting started around 5:00 a.m. When I finally get up, Maeve winds around my ankles, which is dangerous at any time of the day, complaining about no food in her dish and the state of the world in general and how she slept.

Galway is a little different. He's the strong, silent type. He just gives me judgmental faces whether or not I deserve it.

I'd left the camper door open, the screen door latched so they could look outside if they wanted, which Maeve appreciated and Galway did not. A woman on her morning walkabout with two small dogs waved and said, *Can I bother you for a minute?*

Sure, I said. There's nothing bothersome about it. I figured she wanted to ask about the Scamp, and those conversations bring me great delight.

We've got the Scamp just up the road there.

Oh! I said. *I saw it when I pulled in. I was going to walk up a little later and see if you were around. It's always fun to see a Scamp cousin.*

She wondered if she could peek inside mine, and I'm always a little thrilled to let people have a look, partially because I'm very proud of what Dad and I have done to the camper and partially because it's participating in the community of Scamps. It's also good incentive to make sure the bed is made and everything put away.

We chatted for a few minutes, and an older woman of retirement age walked up with her two dogs, and I'd seen her walking her dogs a few times before. The three of us stood in the shade.

Is it just you? she asked.

Me and the cats, I said as the first one said she needs to get going. They were pulling out today.

The second one smiled. *I wondered,* she said. *There are a bunch of us Sisters on the Fly up there. Have you heard of the group before?*

I had. It's a national organization of solo women campers, but I'd never done more than click on their website.

There were five or six women camping alone together for the weekend, she told me, and invited me up to join them later in the afternoon or evening to meet them. She said, *The only rules for Sisters on the Fly are (1) no husbands or kids on the trips; (2) be kind.* I grinned.

I went back and forth about joining them all day, because socializing with strangers never seems like fun, but after the second tornado siren went off and the storm passed, I was in a particular mood where I could handle small talk with a gaggle of strangers. The storms had not made a dent in the humidity, but at least the temperatures were a bit more manageable.

I filled my water bottle and walked up the road to where they were all enjoying a pineapple upside-down cake made in a Dutch oven over the fire. Their first experiment, they said. It was good. They made space for me at the picnic table.

They asked cursory questions, the kind strangers do when you're getting to know somebody new, about how long I'd been camping, how long I'd been camping alone, and jokingly apologized for the presence of one of their husbands, who had shown up accidentally. I wasn't quite sure what the story there was, but it seemed like there was one. They asked me what I do for a living, I told them I taught English, they wanted to know what level, and I said college.

Wow, said the husband.

You're always surprised by the education level the Sisters have and what we do, said his wife, and it wasn't the kindest tone of voice. Clearly there was history of some sort there, and I thought about what we assume about women who camp, who camp solo, and what their reasons for doing so are, and what lives they have built. There's still this Benevolent Sexism of the Road that doesn't recognize that this man's astonishment over my education, or my job, or the fact I've been camping alone for years bordered on insulting. Maybe it's that it feels almost aggressive, like a deliberate refusal to understand how toxic his thinking is—and I would bet he'd be deeply confused to be called out on it. He seemed like a nice guy, yet he had no idea how his compliment would be perceived—and would be shocked that it didn't land as he intended.

And yet, even as I swallowed my irritation, knowing that *he doesn't mean anything by it,* I thought about how women are conditioned to excuse this kind of thinking as *oh, he's just like that* or *oh, he's just from a different generation,* or ignore it entirely rather than feeling anger, or call it out and make the man in question uncomfortable for what he said. So even if I didn't know where his wife's specific irritation came from, I knew where it came from generally. These women had likely faced the same sexism I had every time they got on the road.

As they tried to sell me on the camaraderie of the Sisters on the Fly, I learned that all the women at this picnic table were married, partnered, or widowed. They told me all about getting together on various weekends to camp solo together and the larger trips to places like Yellowstone that the national organization was planning. I nodded politely, definitely certain that I was in good company, that I was among women who, should we camp together, would not treat me like an idiot. These were women who were doing what I did—setting up and tearing down their campers by themselves, dealing with flat tires and faulty converters and finicky appliances. They knew that the only reason God invented shins was so that we could find our trailer hitches in the dark.

You should check us out and think about joining, the women told me before I headed back to the Scamp for the night, thinking about what we know as women, what we know as camping women, and what we know as solo camping women.

I will, I said, knowing that I probably wouldn't but appreciating the invitation anyway.

———

ALONE AT THE TOP OF KAKABEKA FALLS IN BRILLIANT morning sunshine, I know I'm standing on unstable shale as I watch how the Kaministiquia River tumbles 130 feet into the gorge it has carved out of Precambrian rock. I wrap myself in all those beautiful syllables. *Kaministiquia*. It's a moment that screams Thomas Merton: "Solitude is not something you must hope for in the future. Rather, it is a deepening of the present, and unless you look for it in the present, you will never find it."

The tops of the trees are tossing their heads like fractious horses. The shale bedrock is eroding before my eyes as the waterfall spiraled and fractured in the morning sun. But in this place, I can recognize how the natural world likes to remind us that we know more than we can verbalize, to trust what we know in our bodies about the way the world works, and I wonder what it will tell me if I can find a way to listen. I also wonder how landscape feeds into anxiety, how the probable mental illness and PTSD of World War I that my great-grandfather tried to leave behind in Maine followed him to San Diego, and how those stories can be read—and heard—in the landscape. He tried to construct stability there, in that little adobe house, in his marriage and children, but instead he passed down further instability. Here, I'm also standing in a place of instability.

I'm spending some time with this idea of embodiment, what our bodies know about the world, natural and otherwise, that our conscious mind cannot translate, because Kakabeka Falls is trying to tell me something, or remind me of something, and it has to do with what I think of as embodied landscapes. Waterfalls are an embodied landscape, I decide. Waterfalls require your whole body in space to be present, to really understand the impact of them. Stillness cannot capture the way a rainbow through the spray moves and shifts in a breeze, the way it smells differently from the top than the base, the water newly full of oxygen and energy. The mist on your skin, the roar of the water.

I have long believed that we carry stories in our bodies, just as the landscape writes its stories into its bedrock, and these stories are no less present for lacking human speech— it's a matter of knowing how we function in a more-than-human world. I first started thinking about this idea back in high school, when my history teacher Mr. Smith told us that there's a color of pink he viscerally cannot stand, because it was the color Jackie was wearing when JFK was shot. I have a similar reaction to the shade of yellow of Jacob Wetterling's sweater in the photograph his family used to plead for his safe return after he was kidnapped in 1989, three days before my eleventh birthday. It's not too much to say that Jacob's kidnapping broke the state of Minnesota, made us fearful in a way we never had been before. But I feel that color yellow in my stomach, along my shoulder blades, even when I see it out of context.

What does our body know that our minds do not?

It seems important to me to know when an experience becomes historical rather than just *in the past*, and I start to wonder if it's when those events are no longer embodied, when we can no longer feel them in our bellies, on our skin. Embodied history, embodied landscapes. What does our body remember that our minds do not? For me, 9/11 will never be history, because the mention of it still puts me in 100-degree Spokane heat and goosebumps. Mr. Smith still feels the assassination of JFK in his gut. For my grandfather, I don't imagine the deaths of his father, mother, and brother were ever historical events, to the point where he never spoke of them in my hearing, not even fun little memories. For him, that grief would always live in his body, would always be present tense, and if it lives in his belly, in his bones, in his cells, did he pass that knowledge down to my dad? Did my dad pass it to me? What do I carry in my genes of murder and suicide and war and depression and *the* Depression and more war and mental illness? For my dad, those events are less a part of his physical experience, and he can talk about them without difficulty. For me, they don't live in my body at all except as sparks of curiosity, the sting of spray from a waterfall on my skin.

I know that the Nova Scotia peninsula moves under the force of the Bay of Fundy's tides, and I think that if I concentrate hard enough, I can feel the stone here at Kakabeka Falls under my feet vibrating with the force of the falls, the muscle memory of a place that remembers things, knows things, and requires no human comprehension to hold its knowledge. My dad's Acadian ancestors came from a place of deep instability, moved across the continent to Southern California, another place of deep instability, and I wonder just how much that factored into their DNA, the literal ways their environments shaped their lives, and how much we now dismiss because we're taught our bodies are not something that can be trusted. The embodied history—and present tense—of women remains complicated.

Women are taught not to trust what they know in their bodies, from being told our pain is normal to having migraines dismissed as just anxiety, to medical misogyny that ignores how heart attack symptoms are different for women, to the persistent argument that the cervix has no nerve endings and so there's no need to offer women pain relief for biopsies or IUDs, to the intense cruelty of the post-Roe world. But I'm adding a new angle to my thinking about what it means to have a female body moving about the world, because the reality is that the road itself is full of gendered danger. The road is not safe for women, and neither is my Jeep. Seat belts were tested on male-sized crash test dummies, and even those intended to simulate women are simply smaller male dummies, which do not take into account the ways that bone density and pelvis location are different. Women are 73 percent more likely to be seriously injured in a car crash, and according to a 2021 article in the *Washington Post*, "a five-star safety rating for a car or truck means it was highly rated for a 5-foot-9-inch, 170-pound man. We have much less information on how safe a car might be for a 5-foot-2-inch, 110-pound woman." I'm five-eight and my seat belt still hits me across the throat. Short women are even more at risk, not just from not being able to reach pedals or being able to see over the dashboard—another thing that has become standard humor around women drivers—but also, weight sensors that would deploy air bags in a crash sometimes don't register small women.

A woman's body on the road is more complicated than jokes about women drivers—which we're still supposed to laugh at—and we still swallow the sexism as just the way the world works. We're supposed to just shrug and move on. Nothing we can do.

Part of this adjustment starts at birth. Most women have been drilled since infancy about being aware of our surroundings and how to manage risk, and here I am on the road, ignoring most of it. There was a sharp contrast between our 1980s rural upbringing, where my sisters and I were turned loose to the outdoors unsupervised as a matter of course, and the constant instruction to *take your sister with you to the bathroom* after Jacob Wetterling was kidnapped, because Stranger Danger was the creature we all feared in the 1980s. It was the era of missing kids on milk cartons, the largely manufactured fear of being snatched off the street, when the statistics revealed that most kidnappings are perpetrated by family members or friends. Maybe I remember more of it than my sisters or was more aware of adults talking about it, or maybe it was that Jacob was so close in me to age. I didn't see much change when I reached adulthood, as many of us still relied on the buddy system or nail polish that detects roofies. After college, our grad classes were held in a building not in the safest part of town, and it was unspoken for the woman who parked closest to the building to drive the others to their cars. How many male friends never noticed we did this or never noticed how we checked the back seat of our cars before getting in or how we clutched our keys between our fingers like claws?

Women on the road have to be self-sufficient to keep ourselves safe. I know how to jump a car and have the jumper cables to do it, but conventional wisdom still holds: *If you need a jump, you have jumper cables. If a strange man needs a jump, you're just a girl who doesn't know what those are.* A man, given the sexism inherent in the system, will never honestly ask a woman for help with a car—they will, like Ted Bundy, however, fake being injured and ask for assistance getting to their vehicle, preying on women's training to be kind and helpful. I now have a battery jump starter so that I don't need another person to help me out. When I packed up the Scamp to head toward the Maritimes without a cell phone, I mentally flipped through all the advice camping women give other women and the structure of safety we create on the road, those who advocate camping with a gun or a protective German shepherd or who put two chairs outside the camper or a worn pair of men's boots outside the door to make it look like we're not alone. I've never done any of it, because it doesn't feel right, but I understand the impulse.

THE MORNING AFTER THE PINEAPPLE-UPSIDE DOWN CAKE with the Sisters on the Fly, I packed up the cats and the camper and drove the hour to the National Archives annex outside of St. Louis, where I had an appointment to view whatever family military records still existed, because I assumed I would find insights into last several generations through their war service. The road to the annex is along the floodplain side of the bluffs, and it was a beautiful drive—and the facility is built into the bluffs itself, which seemed right, somehow. There was plenty of room for me to park the Jeep and Scamp, so I cracked the windows for the cats and headed inside, where it was cool and quiet. There's something intensely comforting about being inside the rock, the bluffs, as if it were forming an exoskeleton around the exposed nerves it held.

I was there to find Bill Sr.'s World War I records, or my grandfather's World War II records, but I learn that only Walt's survive, because the 1973 fire burned so many of the records. Walt's survived because he was a Marine and those records were stored elsewhere. With Walt's military folder in my hand, the room quiet and sterile, I opened it to find his death certificate, which, as I expected, read homicide, and now I cannot separate the emotional chill from the physical chill in my memory.

But then:

Cause of Death: hemopericardium.
Due to or consequence of: laceration, heart and aorta.
Due to or consequence of: stab wound, chest.
Describe how injury occurred: stabbed in chest with unknown weapon, by unknown person.

And yet this person is not unknown. I knew these things, but the goosebumps on my skin as I read further spoke of a different story, of what my body knew that I

81

didn't. Something about being inside the protective bluffs of the National Archives annex, with the shell between me and the world a solid and unmoving boundary of stone, had me thinking about being hard-hearted, and how that stone was holding a different pitch for me right now in this place. I read that scientists have discovered that Castleton Tower in Utah vibrates at the same pitch as a human heartbeat, matching a landscape to the human animals on it. I'd like to know what that feels like someday. We like to locate what we feel emotionally in our chests, in our heart, when that's scientifically inaccurate. I think about echoes, about vibrations inside us and out, I wonder if that contributes to the landscapes that we feel something in, feel calmed, feel at home, or conversely, feel on edge.

I wonder about the stories I'm headed toward, the stories that the landscape knows, the ones the Babines left behind on the shores of the Bay of Fundy that can't be heard from a distance. The one story I actually knew about Acadie before I left was not written by an Acadian but by Longfellow. It didn't escape me, as I reread *Evangeline*, that it was *Evangeline* who went in search of Gabriel. It's *her* one-sided story of closure, of restoration, not his. *She's* on the road; *she's* the one traveling. I read *Evangeline* with deep irritation as Gabriel continued to elude her, moving away from her, not toward her. The story is supposed to be romantic, tragic, when it's just a terrible, awful story of pursuing a love, chasing a relationship, when it's one-sided. It seems important to consider at this point, here at Kakabeka Falls, *how do we tell a story?*

And what happens when others tell the story for us?

CHAPTER FIVE

MAYBE I SHOULD HAVE SUSPECTED THAT THE DRIVE from Thunder Bay to Sault Ste. Marie wouldn't go as planned when the morning started out with A MOOSE on the side of the road, just standing there like a "discarded early draft of an idea for an animal," as the essayist Paul Gruchow once described them. I can't remember if I've ever seen a moose before in the wild—I don't think I have—and it's really easy to forget how enormous they are until the next time I watch the opening credits of *Northern Exposure*. I wish I could have gotten a picture of it, just standing there peacefully in the ditch watching the world and a weirdly shaped camper go by, but that doesn't happen when you're at speed and you're well past the moose before you figure out you're not hallucinating.

I'm not hallucinating. Oh, my god, that was A MOOSE!

The cats are not impressed, and this strikes me as one of the principal irritations of traveling and camping alone: the collective, shared exclamation of *did you see that?*—and there's literally nobody to share it with. I won't say that the moose was as clichéd a moment as *we're not in Minnesota anymore, Maeve*, but it was close.

I left Kakabeka Falls about 7:45 a.m., and my main goal was to keep an eye on the gas tank en route to Sault Ste. Marie, which would take me about eight hours. This was The Plan and I planned it very carefully, because having A Plan is the principal way I manage being on the road alone. Everything is managed down to the smallest detail with color-coded Post-it notes. There isn't a whole lot of sightseeing or good reasons to stop between Thunder Bay and Sault Ste. Marie, so I decided to push through. It would be a long, ugly day of driving, but there were no good alternatives. I ate my oatmeal, filled my big green Stanley thermos with very strong Earl Grey, put the cats in their kennels, broke camp, and headed out. Maeve vomited before we got to the gates of the park, as per usual, so at least I had a handy trash can ready.

Death, taxes, Maeve.

Galway stared judgmentally from his kennel on the front seat.

We were off to a good start. Traveling with cats is an adventure.

The status of the gas tank was a priority. Yesterday, I went in search of gas and could not get either my credit or debit card to work, and my anxiety increased to the point where I thought I could feel electricity in the ends of my hair. Later I would realize that the fear fizzing in my blood was not one of actual physical danger, but a much more psychologically gendered fear. I'm not afraid on the road in a physical way, but I'm fighting a fear of failure, a fear of looking like an idiot, a fear of running out of gas on the side of the road and facing the snark often aimed at women drivers. It's as potent a fear as any other. I fear problems and conundrums that I can't think my way out of, because as a solo person, if I can't do it, it doesn't get done. I'd rather drive well-traveled roads to get where I'm going than the scenic route, because to be truly alone with no way to access help is my greatest fear.

I went to a different gas station and the card reader still didn't like my card—and so with increasing desperation, with the stress starting to create that tunnel vision I recognized, I went inside. I was running out of gas and I only had American dollars.

It must have shown on my face.

No problem, the cashier said. *Just pump your gas and we'll call the bank if we need to.*

The adrenaline rush of relief made my fingers tingle. *Okay,* I said. *Thank you.*

I filled the tank and put some fifty liters in—$80 worth— and inside the store the cashier ran my card, and it worked fine. Maybe it helped that the cashier was female, that the panic of the morning's hunt for gas had been so easily solved, but the answer to the problem was that Canada had switched to chip cards, which would not become common in the States for another year or two. It was a moment of relief so intense that I could feel tears building in my chest. I resolved never to let this happen again.

From the back seat, Maeve snarked that this was twice in the last couple of days that I had lost my mind over gas, first in Two Harbors and then again today.

I said her commentary was unnecessary.

———

ABOUT 1:00 P.M., I'M IN WAWA, WHICH IS ABOUT HALFWAY to Sault Ste. Marie, and the sign says that the 17 is closed south of Wawa for emergency repairs. There are sinkholes in the road. There's a detour, so instead of three hours left in my day, I'm looking at least four and a half. *On an old logging road*, the nice young lady at the visitor's center tells me, but I don't really know what that means. That's uncomfortable, but what's the alternative? I'd already seen some spectacular scenery, granite and gorges and the kind of impact I'd forgotten that landscapes could have. I've been living on the Great Plains in Nebraska and on the Red River Valley of Minnesota–North Dakota for the last several years, and have learned to appreciate the scope of that particular landscape, so it is necessary to have my senses recalibrated. The sun is bright, the sky is blue, I have snacks and tea and water and a porta-potty, and other than the basic inconvenience of it all, there is no reason to get overly upset about a detour. We don't tell stories about the things that went well, after all. I'm on a road trip, an adventure. This is all part of what comes with putting wheels to the road, even if I had A Plan.

The moose should have been a sign.

———

WHAT I LEARN ON THIS DAY DRIVING THE DETOUR FROM Thunder Bay is that *old logging road* means narrow, winding, and at turns, straight-up terrifying, as I try to match the speed I feel safest pulling a camper against the giant trucks tucked up against the Scamp's butt who want to go faster. Under normal circumstances, I'd pull off on the side of the road to let them pass, because I have been taught the etiquette of the road from a young age.

The road has no shoulders.

No margin for error, not even inches.

When the Scamp, the cats, and I get to the tiny town of Chapleau, I pass it, thinking I'm okay on gas, but then a very small sign tells me there would be no gas for 120 kilometers, so I turn around—make a U-turn in the middle of the road with a camper, which I'm very proud of—and I go back and fill up the tank. This turns out to be a very good idea. There is no way I would have made it to Thessalon without a full gas tank, and I relearn this important lesson of the road: never let the gas tank go below a third of a tank. This is usually advice I follow in the winter, not in the summer.

I'm fairly sure that the rivers, the trees, the wildflowers, the steepness of the hillsides painted in dappled sun are beautiful, but I don't really notice as I white-knuckle the steering wheel, tunnel vision tight around my ears. I'm pretty sure that what I'm not looking at hasn't changed in several hundred thousand years, like *there's the planet's fingerprints* right in front of me, but now's not a good time to look, or think much about anything that's not straight out my windshield or in my rearview—and intellectually I know why: on one of our early family trips, we rented our friend's pop-up and took it to Winnipeg, where the camper came off the Blazer's hitch in the middle of Winnipeg traffic, and even though I know intellectually that my dad had the wrong size ball for the hitch, it's a sense memory I can't shake when I'm pulling the Scamp, even though I *know* the hitch ball is the right size, that it's locked down tight and *there's no way* it's coming loose—*I know this*—and Dad taught me from the beginning to *always cross the safety chains*, though at the time he swears he told me it's to catch the hitch if it comes off, and Winnipeg was twenty years ago, and this should not be a thing lodged in my belly, but

I'm carrying this fear nonetheless, right there, sharp under my ribs. I don't even remember the event itself, *so how do we carry things we don't remember?*

He says later, *I hope when you remember it, you just remember that I never lost my cool. And I got to buy a new crescent wrench to fix it.*

I don't actually remember it at all, I say. *I remember the experience of it, not the event.*

My body remembers it, but my mind doesn't. I've learned the lesson of Winnipeg, but on this particular road, I don't know if the lesson will hold.

———

I cross the line between the Arctic watershed and the Atlantic watershed a couple of times, my knuckles white on the steering wheel, sun sliding and dancing through the canopy of trees on both sides of Ye Olde Logging Road. The Laurentian Divide is the Northern Divide, the point at which water north of this point flows up to Hudson Bay. Water south of this point flows toward the Gulf of Mexico—or, given that I'm directly north of the Great Lakes, water flows toward the Gulf of St. Lawrence. I've passed continental divides many times before, but I've only noticed the east–west. I feel a little silly to realize I never considered they might exist north–south as well, given how much time I've spent on the Red River of the North in Fargo–Moorhead, waiting for the spring thaws to trigger a flood. The Laurentian Divide goes through Lake Traverse, and the Bois de Sioux River flows north from the lake, and what will become the Minnesota River flows south from the lake. Then it zigzags north of Lake Superior, so that its watershed flows south.

I find these dividing lines compelling. I wonder, too, about this Acadian Babine patrilineal line I'm driving toward, fathers and brothers, and how the women I descended from disappear, how hard it is to trace their lines, how much I wondered about them. I look at the records I find of the women marrying at fifteen or sixteen, bearing ten or twelve or fourteen children until their husbands died, and then they remarried and continued to bear more children. And yet, the lines I can follow are male, and this family of men descends into a constellation of women and girls and mothers and women who choose not to become mothers and who instead buy a small camper to explore a world that is full of curiosities.

I know that the land I'm driving toward, the land my great-grandfather left, moves twice a day under the force of the Bay of Fundy's tides. It's delightfully paradoxical to be driving toward a place that is a family origin point, a family-historical fixed point that is not exactly fixed to its landscape, a journey in reverse. I know where we *are*, but I don't know how *where we were* influenced who we were before my great-grandfather Bill Sr. moved to a land of earthquakes and winds and wildfires. There's a photograph of the family in the late 1930s, and characteristically, my grandfather is taking this very seriously while Walt is grinning. But I grew up in the land of the Canadian Shield, and the land I'm driving across now is the oldest exposed land on the planet, some of which is as old as 4.2 billion years, the rock bare like an exposed nerve, too sensitive. The glaciers of the last ice age scraped it clean to the bedrock, carving grooves into the surface, laying its mark.

This isn't land that moves. This is land that other things move across.

CHAPTER SIX

AND THEN, A BEAR.

Sitting on the side of the road. Another moment of *holy shit, was that a bear? THAT WAS A BEAR!* I've seen bears in the wild before, and they're the derpiest animals, galumphing their way from one place to another without anything that resembles grace but still somehow liquid in their movements. The cats are uninterested in local wildlife, and I might be getting a little punch-drunk after so long in the Jeep, so much energy focused on the road ahead of me, the sharp inclines inches from the edge of the road. Mistakes on this road will not be easy to recover from, and I'm still alone. The bear is more exciting in the experience than the event, and it's a good reminder of the wildness I'm driving through.

This is their territory.

I'm the stranger here, the one who doesn't belong.

About 7:45 p.m., it's still light when I get back to the safety of the 17, east of Sault Ste. Marie in Thessalon, and I pull off the road to get my Good Sam campground directory out of the Scamp to find a campground, *but the handle on the Scamp's door will not budge,* and I am terrified in that way you get when you're overly tired and overly stressed, with low blood sugar, and unable to process the simplest things. It's a moment of the purest panic I've ever felt, that the trip would be over before it started, that I am not as capable as I believed myself to be, that no amount of planning would ever make such an undertaking successful, and that voice in the back of my brain warning me that *this was all a terrible idea* gets louder.

Maeve's commentary from the back seat does not help.

When I get myself together, take a deep breath, or two, and take comfort in the fact that it's still light out, it's not raining, I am able to get creative—and I realize that I hadn't locked the back window of the Scamp, so I slide the window and screen free and climb up the back bumper and wiggle my way into the camper head first, hoping nobody is watching my legs hanging out the back of the camper as I try to get in. *Graceful* is not an option. I try to open the door from inside with no luck, which results in more deep breathing exercises.

What am I going to do if my door is broken?

What I wouldn't know for several more years is that Ye Old Logging Road probably cracked the fiberglass near the doorframe, which would require extensive repair once I could no longer use a bungee cord to keep the door closed on the road—but once fixed, it would be good as new. Fiberglass is amazing.

I decide to leave the door for now and grab the Good Sam directory, find a campground. The owner is very nice and yes, they've just opened for the season and have plenty of space. Thank God. On a weekday in late May, it's pretty easy to find a campsite. She leads me to my site and kindly assists me in figuring out the door—I have to push in and pull up to manage the latch—and *then the mosquitoes descend.*

Hoards of them.

Legions.

Mythic numbers.

I'm from Minnesota. I know mosquitoes. This was something else entirely.

I set the camper up as fast as I can, but the universe is against speed. The electricity in my site isn't working, so I have to pull out my bright orange extension cord and hook it into the empty site next to me. While I have leather work gloves that I generally use to set up the camper, I prefer the gardening gloves with latex coating over the palms and fingers, as they give me a much more solid grip to pull down the jacks when they're being stubborn. Of course, they're being stubborn when I'm trying to move quickly, but I'm prepared. Dad would never let me out into the world without duct tape and WD-40.

If it moves and it shouldn't, duct tape; if it doesn't move and it should, WD-40.

I'm sure that was a lesson I learned by kindergarten.

The water is not working in my site or the next one, which generally isn't the biggest deal, because I don't have a bathroom in my camper and don't generally hook up to water—I do fill up my Brita for drinking water when I stop for the day. *Fine, no water. Uncomfortable, but not the end of the world; I'll figure it all out tomorrow. I'm fine for now.* Still trying to set up the camper quickly before darkness descends completely, dodging bird-sized mosquitoes that are getting bigger by the moment, I go into the bath house, and there isn't any running water in there either, not in the tap, the toilet, or the shower. I am tired enough not to get back in the Jeep and question the campground host about it. I have a jug of water in the Jeep and a porta-potty, so my

immediate needs are not at risk. I don't have enough energy
to care about more than that. *I'm fine for now; I'm safe; we
all made it through today in one piece and that's all that matters
right now.* In the morning, I will resolve to never take the
basic necessities for granted again. I'll always keep water on
hand, and food that doesn't need to be cooked over a fire.

Once the jacks are finally down, the camper stabilized,
and the cats transferred from their kennels to the camper, I
slam the door behind me and take stock. The rat fur cover-
ing the walls and roof is solid with mosquitoes—I've never
seen anything like it.

The swarm is now inside the camper.

I turn on the air conditioning fan to keep the air moving enough so that they can't land, and then I take a video
of Galway, he who is afraid of everything, sitting on the
bed, swatting mosquitoes with his little clawless paw.
When given the chance, my mighty mosquito hunter dives
under the covers. For the most part, the moving air works
well enough and the three of us sleep better than I expect
to. *We're safe. We're fine.* We were never in true danger today, but it feels like I escaped something nonetheless, and I
wonder how I'll tell this story when I get home.

———

IT WAS EASY ENOUGH TO START THE RESEARCH INTO THE
Acadian side of the family, even though my grandfather
didn't give me much to work with. Given records easily
available online, I knew that my great-grandfather William
Henry Babine Sr. was born in Nova Scotia in 1889, and I'm
not sure where and how the rest of the initial information
came from, but I suspect most of the information came from

various American census records. Place of birth, occupation, immigration dates, family members. I fleshed out the first umbrella of the tree: Bill Sr. and his siblings, their parents. Maine, Massachusetts. Typing *Babine* into Ancestry's search engine would lead to other breadcrumbs, and I started to piece things together, one name and date and place-name at a time. Once I finally splurged and bought the worldwide subscription to Ancestry sometime in my midtwenties, I was able to dig into the Canadian records to go back further. Sometimes it was a matter of clicking on public trees that contained names I recognized, just to see what they'd found.

I started developing my own ethics to this online archival work: I could only add these people to my tree if I found the records themselves. So, I might find siblings I didn't know about on a random family tree on Ancestry or WikiTree, but I'd have to find the census records for myself to confirm before I'd allow myself to add them to my tree, because most of that information is wrong. I'm not always consistent here, especially when combining what little knowledge I have with the data, but it's my goal. If there's no clear answer to the accuracy, it's valuable to know that. Not knowing can be as valuable as certainty in the scheme of things.

Because my memory is largely spatial, when I started creating the spiderweb of direct descendants, I could follow the map in my mind like it was hanging in front of me. Context was a little harder to come by, because history stretched and pulled, because data can't contain nuance. Port-Royal, later renamed Annapolis Royal, was established in 1605 as the first settlement in Acadie, and then nine major wars would be fought with Nova Scotia as their theater. On the gray day I will arrive to tour it, two weeks from now, the reproduction of the original settlement at the Port-Royal National Historic Site will feel like it would have been bustling with rough-hewn men who haven't seen a bath in too many weeks, rough-hewn buildings that I imagine provided shelter, but not comfort, against a Maritime winter. It was not intended to be a colony, simply a trading outpost. The promotional material for the place is so delighted that "Costumed interpreters share with visitors the challenges faced by the French, and their friendship with the Mi'kmaq." I look at my family tree and see my eleven-greats grandfather Pierre LeJeune[11] married an "unknown Micmac [sic] woman," and their daughter, my ten-greats grandmother, Edmee[10], was born in 1624, about the time the Acadian settlement became more permanent. According to other sources like Acadian.org, though, "There is too much controversy with this family to state anything as a fact that cannot be proven by a reliable source." Pierre LeJeune[11] may not even be Edmee's father, and maybe my outrage about her parentage is unfounded. The uncertainty doesn't bother me, because I know the intermarrying was common enough—and the Acadian population small enough—that I'm sure somebody I'm related to took a First Nations wife. When the trading monopoly was canceled in 1610 and most of the settlers went home to France, some of them stayed with the Mi'kmaq.

I juggle French and English colonies in my mind, which somehow all look like Colonial Williamsburg as viewed from my teenage memory from our 1994 camping trip to Washington, DC—all fichus and fifes, the wax seal I bought as a souvenir but never managed to use correctly, the stocks and pillories my sisters and I took pictures in and were only too happy to be released from, the box maze so gloriously precise and orderly.

How in the world did you raise three kids who actually liked that kind of stuff? I asked my dad once. *How did we not complain that it was boring?*

I have no idea, he answered, baffled. *But I'm really glad for it.*

It just doesn't make sense to me, I said. *I just don't know how you did it.*

Me either, he said.

I wondered if it was partially because my parents and Minnesota grandparents instilled in us a particular curiosity about the world, perhaps because my mother and her parents were teachers, and storytelling was how they best understood the world. Our family certainly wasn't perfect—and isn't—but my parents and Minnesota grandparents did many things I'm grateful for. Gram told great stories of people and places, planted them in our imaginations, so that when I found the letter her older sister Harriet had written from Washington, DC, in 1945, standing in the street to watch the caisson carrying FDR's coffin pass by, it brought real people in past times into my present. Gram's stories of her college roommate, Masako, who was Nisei, took internment camps off the pages of textbooks and put them into real human terms. These were the kind of stories I wished the California Grandparents would tell, the kind that put life back into history.

On our family trips, we didn't make a regular habit of amusement parks, likely because they were too expensive, but we did go to Disneyland once—and it was a huge treat, though my enduring memory of it is not the opening of the brand new Star Tours ride, for which we stood in line for three hours, but a simmering kind of righteous anger of an eight-year-old because my mother made me wear a tank top instead of a T-shirt, over my objections about getting sun-burned. We also went to SeaWorld in San Diego, where I got shit on by a dyspeptic seagull at the killer whale show, marking the beginning of many years where my father would yell *seagull!* just to watch me dive for cover. It soured my later experience of SeaWorld in Ohio, where Kim begged to go after becoming obsessed with being a killer whale trainer when she grew up. She told me, "I'm pretty sure I said, 'If we don't go, you're not supporting my dreams!'" which was a hilariously dramatic position for her to take. We did go, and she took home a stuffed killer whale (later named Lombard for the crooked street in San Francisco).

Colonial Williamsburg was founded in 1632, about the same time my ancestors came to Acadie, which might be why my memory resurrected it from deep in my teenage years. Colonial Williamsburg, as a restoration and reproduction, represents the eighteenth-century ambitions of the place, and I wonder what a full restoration of Port-Royal would have looked like from an Acadian view. In 1713, the Treaty of Utrecht made Acadie permanently British territory—*Nova Scotia*—and it's sometimes considered the fourteenth American colony, because the Declaration of Independence is still two generations away. In 1755, the British, proba-bly deeply sick of dealing with rebellious Irish Catholics in Ireland, finally had the military power to force the issue with the "French Neutrals," as the Acadians were called, and when the Catholic Acadians refused to take the Oath of Allegiance and swear that the English monarch was the head of the church, they were taken from their homes and tossed onto ships bound for anywhere, and loyal English planters were given their lands. *Le Grand Dérangement*—it went by many names in English, the Great Upheaval, the Great Disturbance, the Expulsion. The Acadians were dumped anywhere the ship was headed, whether it was Maryland, South Carolina, or any of the other American colonies—and because they were French, because they were Catholic, they were not only not welcomed, in some places, they were not even allowed off the ships. Ten thousand were expelled; thousands died of disease or in shipwrecks. I bought a map at the Grand-Pré National Historic Site that represents the waves of deportations in wide swaths of colors that resemble an arrow pointing to their destination. The map, like all the others of my collection representing a place out of time, is out of context.

In 1767, my seven-greats grandfather, Joseph Babin[7], and three of his younger children, Cyprien, Etienne, and Elizabeth (his wife, Anne Marie Landry[7], and the rest of his family having died in Maryland), got on a boat headed for Louisiana. I don't know why they chose to join Acadians in Louisiana—whose name linguistically deteriorated from Acadian to Cajun—rather than go back to Nova Scotia. Maybe they assumed the rest of their family was dead and there was nothing to go back to.

But here's what I fixate on: On the 1767 Louisiana census, Joseph[7], Cyprien, Etienne, and Elizabeth are all listed in the Spanish forms of their names. I stare at the list for a moment, not comprehending—and then it dawns, with embarrassing clarity. It was still Spanish Louisiana. The Louisiana Purchase wouldn't happen until 1803. It's a moment where time exists in a funny way, history functioning on separate timelines in my mind, and it takes deliberate effort to remember that it didn't happen in separate strands of experience. What surprises me about this is how surprised I am, how time functions in history, that it functions like an accordion, with years and events on the pleats, close to each other when collapsed, but so far apart when expanded. There are a lot of metaphors in my head for how I'm trying to understand timescapes, landscapes, like how distance measured *as the crow flies* is different than how long it will take to reach a destination by vehicle.

I wonder what my seven-greats grandparents, Joseph Babin[7] and Anne Marie Landry[7], talked about at the dinner table as the rumblings of trouble were getting louder. I wonder about Joseph[7] sitting at the table with his own brothers, and I wonder if they resembled my grandfather, my father, his siblings: the dark hair, the build of their shoulders. Twentieth-century military records describe the Babine men as dark, dark hair, dark complexions, and I wonder, if I saw Joseph[7] and his brothers sitting together, would I recognize them as my blood? Joseph and Anne Marie's oldest two sons, my six-greats grandfather Pierre[6] and his brother Joseph, would have been in their midtwenties, likely fully involved in any discussions of resistance. Their sister Elizabeth would have been in her teens, brothers Etienne and Cyprien younger. *What do we do? What if they come for us? When will they come for us?*

I wonder about their nightly prayers, the candles they lit to find their friends and relatives.

⸻

WHEN I WAS IN THIRD GRADE, THE CALIFORNIA Grandparents came to visit us in Minnesota, and I remember asking both my grandmothers how they were related and not completely understanding that they were related to me, but not to each other. It didn't quite make sense, since they were both my grandmothers. We think of DNA as the key that will unlock everything, a map, a path to understanding this complex line of humans that we come from. My dad and his siblings, including my aunt, who is the youngest, are over six feet tall. My dad, who is six-five, is not the tallest; Uncle Ted is six-seven. They are easily recognizable as related: the same stance, the same black hair, the skin tone this side of ruddy. Each of the brothers laughs like my grandfather. Sometimes I catch my dad out of the corner of my eye, standing in the same bent-at-the-hip stance as Grandpa, and I have to reorient myself, especially as my dad's hair edges from black into silver.

Aunt Teresa's face has fined down to resemble Marion, startlingly so. Looking at my cousins, Laura resembles her father and Jae looks like their mother at that age, particularly the photograph of my teenage aunt, dark haired and beautiful in pale blue at my parents' wedding in 1976. It's easy to take photographs—and DNA—as proof of something, something concrete in how the world is ordered, but it's putting trust in the wrong thing. At the last family reunion, Laura, who was nineteen and six-three, commented how much she likes these kind of gatherings, because it's the only time she feels short. Same goes for her younger sibling, Jae, who was fourteen and six-two. My sisters and I resemble each other, the same pale skin, the same blue-green eyes, the same height, but I don't think we look like either of our parents. Other people have told us there's a strong resemblance, but I can't see it and I don't know why. When Kristi's kids are born, there's a fizz in my blood when I recognize my face in theirs, in Kim's features, a recognition that my bones feel is important.

Forensic crime shows have conditioned us to believe that DNA will answer all our questions, solve all the crimes and questions, and quickly. When it comes to civilian DNA mapping, it's easy to forget that it's based on so little data as to be functionally useless, that my own DNA test places my history in Nova Scotia, though the English, Swedish, and German DNA is not clear as it should be. Kim had hers done and most of her DNA is in eastern Europe, which doesn't make a lot of sense, unless most of her DNA comes down from my paternal grandfather's mother, whose German family came from closer to Poland, not the North Sea. My mother's father was 100 percent German and her mother was 100 percent Swedish, but my mother's DNA isn't 50/50—that's not the way DNA works. Currently my pie chart lists me as 57 percent Swedish, but that seems to change weekly, so I don't put a lot of stock in it. My maternal grandfather was fully German, yet Ancestry says my DNA is only 4 percent German.

DNA—and this belief that DNA is the answer—is tricky. There was a point in my early internet research in the late 1990s or early 2000s when I stumbled on a family tree created by a woman named Celese Peters, who has been working on her family tree for decades, a tree that at the time I found it contained 98,000 names. I was in college. As I poked through her tree, there were no Babins, but I located my six-greats grandfather Pierre Surette[6] (born 1709) and his descendants—which stopped several generations before it got to me—and so I followed Pierre[6] back. And back. *Click. Click.* Further back than I ever thought it would go. With each generation I became more excited.

Then confused.

And wary.

And then skeptical.

Then sarcastic.

Here's why: Pierre Surette's[6] grandmother's name was Jeanne Savoie[8], and as I kept going, I watched the Surettes disappear into the Savoys, to Jeanne's grandparents, who were listed as Prince Tomaso Francesco Savoy[10] and Princess Marie Conde Soissonde Bourbon[10] of France. I rode the natural adrenaline spike at royal titles, because that's objectively neat, but I shoved it aside for a while, until I found that the Savoys were the longest-ruling royal family in Europe. For all my historical interest, I don't have a good handle on European history outside England and Ireland, and I don't have a good handle on royal comings and goings. I tend to compartmentalize history to the point that, when doing my Acadian research, I often forgot that the American Revolution was just decades away from taking shape. It worked better if I could disassociate the *history* from my *family*—though it seemed like the opposite should be true. But I do wonder why we are so quick to connect to the DNA of royalty and ignore the much closer history of murder.

This is wild, I thought, as I watched the seventeenth century disappear into the sixteenth. Then the fifteenth.

Jeanne's great-grandfather was the Duke of Savoy, as were the rest of the paternal ancestors. Savoie, Savoy. The light of a candle lit the Dark Ages of my memory as I kept tracing the name back further through the tree. Sometimes the given names were Italian, sometimes they were French. *Fourteenth century.* I knew the name. *Why did the name seem familiar?* The candle wasn't light enough to determine the answer, so I kept going, with the requisite Wikipedia pages open in a different tab.

Turin, Italy.

Chambéry, France.

I knew those places. *How did I know them?* And then I knew. Because I knew this episode of *History's Mysteries* by heart.

Holy shit.

The Shroud of Turin. My family owned the freaking Shroud of Turin.

Bad choice of wording for my exclamation of surprise and disbelief, I decided as my brain clicked into familiar historical territory. *Not literally holy shit, but close enough?* The Savoy family, whose territory included a huge chunk of Europe, including parts of France and Italy, bought the shroud from Margaret de Charny in the 1450s. The Savoy family seat is in Chambéry, France, and it was Chambéry Cathedral that burned in 1532 with the shroud inside, the event that some use to explain away the shroud's carbon dating results. And, as the story goes, when the cardinal was going to walk from Milan to France to see the shroud and give thanks, the family installed it at Turin Cathedral, also part of the Savoy family territory, where the shroud has been ever since.

This can't be right. The Savoys, being a royal family themselves, intermarried with the other royal houses of Europe, as one does. According to the tree, the Babines are directly descended from King Henry II and Catherine de Medici, as well as Henry's brother François I. We can trace direct descent back to King Felipe II of Spain. The Savoys on Celese's tree go back to 1065. On another line, I've traced the line back to Charlemagne, who is thirty-two generations away from me.

That plus a couple of bucks will get me a nice cup of tea, the rational historian on my shoulder reminded me. It was like playing with Monopoly money. I could hold it in my hands, but it wasn't worth anything. I didn't like the feeling that what I'd done here had turned my curiosity into a version of *Jeopardy!* In fact, even if this information proved to be accurate, my ethics of being the family historian meant that I could really only add it to my own tree if I found the primary documents for myself—and I hadn't done that work yet. What research I have done suggests that it's weird to revise my idea of my father's history and who we were, what we did, how we've come to stand at a different place on the road, and where that road has been. Apparently, there is no solid evidence that the father of Jeanne Savoy[8], François[9], is the son of Tomaso Francesco Savoie[10], and both sides of this genealogical debate are very heated in their opinions: on one hand we have the *get over it, you're not royalty* side, and on the other we have the *just because there's no written proof, that doesn't discount the oral history* side. Most of the speculation is that François is Tomaso's illegitimate son, but there's no record of him anywhere. Several sites speculate that François's parents had a morganatic marriage, which sometimes happens when spouses are of unequal rank (like if one is the Duke of Savoy); the effect is that the spouse and children of the marriage have no claim on the higher-ranked parent's title or possessions. Morganatic marriages seem so fifteenth century, when many of the current European royals have married commoners of no noble rank, though there are a few families for whom marrying of equal rank is required. I suppose a morganatic marriage could explain why François left Sardinia to make something of himself in Acadie: because he couldn't inherit. But it's all speculation at this point, deviating from fact back to the imagination where I started, without records and data to support it.

I did spend some time with Antoine Babin[9], though, the first Babin in Acadie. I can trace my line back to him, back to France where he married Marie Mercier[9], who was nearly twenty years his junior, but then the line disappears. The historical stories of my family's movement—and how that translates to our movement these days—it all seems to be related, and it seems to be important to mark our place in a trail that's been trod for centuries, to wonder how this wanderlust trickled down through Antoine's descendants, movement chosen and forced, descendants that still find it very hard to stay in one place for very long, who still wonder about where they've been and where they go from here.

Maybe this is why my grandfather, instead of telling me anything about his Army service during World War II when I asked, handed me a book about the history of his unit. When he died, it was the first I'd heard about his Purple Heart and Bronze Star earned at the Battle of the Bulge. It was as close to his stories as I was going to get, but I also understood why he never told them. They probably hurt too much.

I think he told the story of the Battle of the Bulge to me and probably Dennis, my dad said. *Since we were military ourselves and could understand. I don't know if he ever talked about it with Ted, Brian, or Teresa.* It's not something that easily comes up in a cozy conversation.

When I learned that my grandfather's military records at the National Archives didn't survive the St. Louis fire, I wasn't ready for that chapter to close.

What's curious to me is that *where do we come from?* is a compelling question at all. I can understand the desire to know *who we come from*, the line of humans who share our blood, so we can know that we're not unmoored in the world, that we're not alone, that we don't stand in this place truly alone, that our dead are never truly dead.

But *who do you come from?* is not the question we ask: we ask *where do you come from?* when we want to know our origins.

CHAPTER SEVEN

AFTER TWO STRANGELY UNEVENTFUL DAYS DRIVING across Ontario, this morning I decide to try for Quebec City and stay for a few days. I'd figured out my route—I wanted to be on the east side of the St. Lawrence River, but that proposition proved more interesting than anticipated, as I'd forgotten just how French Quebec is. Trying to figure out road signs in French when one does not speak French is fairly difficult.

By the time I get to Montreal, I've basically figured out the signs, but then I hit road construction. Hardcore road construction with torn up roads and bypasses and detours, the nasty kind, rather than the slightly inconvenient kind.

And then it starts to storm.

Hard.

Hard enough that the wipers couldn't keep up.

Oh my god.

I have never been so terrified while driving.

That includes pulling the Scamp through Chicago at rush hour.

And Ye Old Logging Road.

I should have known not to trust those easy days on the road. They always come home to roost.

I arrive at the Camping Transit campground outside of Quebec City in the midafternoon, and the man who checks me in and shows me to my campsite offers to back in the camper for me. I swallow my disgust and thank him politely, say *I can do it* through gritted teeth. I back in the Scamp on the first try like a goddamn badass and don't even try to disguise my smug satisfaction as he watches me do it, then tootles away in his little golf cart.

Nobody ever asks my dad if he'd like somebody else to back in his camper.

So I'm in a foul mood.

Most things weren't gendered in our house when we were growing up, probably a function of my dad only having girls and our interest in spending time with him, no matter what he was doing. The household split was gendered, though, in that Dad often took care of the outside things and Mom often took care of the inside tasks, common to their generation, but he was just as likely to cook and do laundry, because he worked three hundred feet from the house and Mom's commute was much longer. He'd also been in the Air Force long enough that he wasn't incompetent at tasks like laundry. When we lived in Laporte, in the years before computers, he and Mom had a deal: she was a faster typer than he was, so she'd type up his sermons on Saturday night, and he mopped the kitchen floor. Once we got a computer, the floor saw a lot less attention.

I've been in this place before, two years ago, and even though I don't plan to retrace my steps in Quebec City, the taste of mushroom and cheese crepes is still fresh on my tongue; the cobblestones of North America's only remaining

THE ALLURE OF ELSEWHERE

walled city are still a shape I feel beneath my feet. It's what I'll wish was still intact when I get to Nova Scotia. As I settle my bones to rest for a few days, there's something about the memory of place that imprinted on me so that I feel a physical oppression of heat and humidity from two years ago, even though right now, the day is mild. My body still knows something about the shape of this place, what it feels like on my skin.

The Camping Transit campground outside of Quebec City is nearly full—I discover it's a group called the Fédération québécoise de camping et de caravaning, a string of words I have no hope of pronouncing correctly, and the adjacent camaraderie feels good. I've spent the first few days of this trip in provincial parks, shielded from neighbors, and here, I'm reminded just how much I like a tiny camper, because the section for water/electric sites is a much more interesting place to be than the fancier water/electric/sewer sites set up for the larger motor homes and trailers. There's a sixteen-foot Scamp here with Quebec plates and an Aliner camper—a hard-sided, triangle-shaped A-frame pop-up—across from me, but I don't talk to either of them. People who camp in smaller campers like mine spend more time outside, hanging around their campfires, reading in their chairs. In my experience, most people who camp in the big Class A motor homes spend most of their time inside. This area of the campground is fairly sparsely populated, but it's nice to be surrounded by the activity of others. In other campgrounds, on other trips, it's been a true, bone-deep pleasure to watch the campground unfold and settle as the afternoon arrivals find their sites.

Setting up is full of routines that have taken on a ritual quality. It's putting out the plastic, red-checked tablecloth on the picnic table—or, as the niblings get older, I'll hand them the tablecloth—and maneuvering the table into a good position. It's finding the best place out of the sun to put my chair and footstool, if it's nice enough to be outside, and rolling out the blue-green striped awning if the wind is calm enough. I haven't used the awning on this trip, because of the weather, and I'm looking forward to using it again, because it changes the shape of the space, adds an outdoor moment to pause, to linger. Later, I'll add some curtains to the awning for further shade and this will become one of my favorite additions to the outdoor living world of the Scamp. I shake out the rug, vacuum up the floor, and wipe it down with a bleach wipe so that my space is clean when I'm done. I've never done that cleaning before I head out, simply because I store wood, boots, and other dirty things on the floor while in transit, and it makes no sense to do that cleaning twice. I fill up the plastic jug with water from the nearby communal water spigot with my handy-dandy water thief that's just an unthreaded rubber adapter I can hook onto a campground's water spigot to fill my jugs without making a mess. I use that jug to fill my Brita and set it on the counter inside. There's good comfort in a routine, the work of making a space, making a life. Everything in the Scamp has a place. I might be in this specific place, a specific campground, but it could have been any of a thousand just like it, from moments spanning back to my childhood, and any number of interchangeable nights.

There's a rhythm to a campground, and it hasn't changed since our parents first packed us in the Starcraft. Evening follows a predictable pattern, settling into its own kinds of rituals and rhythms, the way the rigs roll in about dinner time, the way that each sets up their campsite, who in the family has which jobs. I remember once at Itasca

State Park, the headwaters of the Mississippi, just sitting under the awning with a can of Sociable hard cider and watching the bustle of the campground. I like seeing how other people travel, what their camping looks like, what they're cooking over their fires and grills, the glow of their coals as they sit around the fire after dark, and there's a small space of time when we're all having an experience together and that's a moment that feels good. We're not alone, even if we're in separate spaces. If it rains, we're all experiencing the same damp; if it's lovely, we're all going to enjoy that in different ways.

I remember how delightfully full that Itasca campground was—a fifth wheel right next to me that seemed to be connected to the Starcraft travel trailer and the Class A across the road, probably a family of ten or twelve all camping together. I watched a family with a pop-up pull in and out of the van jumped four young kids. One helped Dad crank up the roof. Another got the bed supports. Another set up chairs around the fire pit. The nostalgia was sweet. I love watching other people camp, how they camp to be together. So much activity—kids on bikes, fires, dinners in progress. I love it all.

It's fairly rare that I encounter other solo campers, but it's certainly becoming more common. I notice who eats inside and who eats outside. Checking out bathrooms, the pool. The kids entertaining themselves, the parents shooing them from the campsite toward the playground, so the adults can get things set up. I remember this from childhood camping— after we'd done our jobs to help set up the camper, we'd head to the playground to create obstacle courses for each other, or Mom would take us to the pool, not just to cool down but to wear us down. That, too, became a ritual.

Only in later years would I notice the ritual of the Evening Walkabout, where people walk around the campground after dinner, ostensibly for exercise for themselves or their dog, but it also serves the purpose of checking out who is here, what they're camping in, cataloging different ways of doing things. The Evening Walkabout is a chance to say hello, to comment on the cuteness of the dogs, those kind of essential small talk moments that aren't actually small talk while in a campground.

Mornings happen in a pattern too. The tents are always up first, cooking breakfast over fires, warming themselves against the chill of morning, before anyone else realizes their circadian rhythms are turning over. The pop-ups are next, especially with children. From there, the more solid your walls and roof, the more likely you are to need an alarm to get up. It's really hard to tune out the movement of the morning when your walls are made of millimeters.

The next morning, I get up just before 7:00 a.m. and notice that one tenting group already has their tent broken down; another—two guys, a baby, and a dog in a campsite with four chairs set up—already has their fire going and it looks like it's nearly down to coals. They've been up for a while. The music they have playing out of the open doors of their ancient Blazer is a little inconsiderate, given the hour on a Sunday morning, but that's normal, too, and it doesn't even cross my mind to complain. The tent across from me is already on a walk with their dog and two kids. They wave and say good morning as I sit at my picnic table with my breakfast of oatmeal and pot of tea, and I raise my mug in salute and smile at them. These are the best camping moments, when I'm not in pursuit of anything or anywhere, just wrapped in the solo life of the road, the stillness of making my own life the way I want it. Galway and Maeve are sitting just inside the screen door, peering out, learning what this morning in Quebec City smells like, how it smells different from yesterday. Of all my personalities, the person I am when I travel is the closest to who I am. I really like who I am when I camp. She's smart and knows what she's doing; she's delightfully sarcastic, takes no shit from anyone or anything, and knows what she wants.

The pop-ups wake up next, about the time I'm ready to refill my little teapot. They don't say good morning as they stumble sleepily past my campsite on the way to the bathrooms, but they do on the way back. I pour more tea and enjoy the scent of the tent's campfire. My mom is right: there really is something marvelous about a morning camp-fire. I don't often have them—and I've had rotten luck with green wood on this trip—but they certainly have a different character than evening fires, when the light dies around you and your eyes adjust to new standards of light and dark. I've missed campground small talk in the early days of this trip, I realize, since the campgrounds have been sparsely popu-lated given how early in the season it is. The dad with two kids and the dog walks by again and the exchange is noth-ing more than *good morning, how are you, glorious morning*, but that's a campground. We don't need more than that, but it's still important.

The campsite is an inviolable space, in that you don't walk across somebody's campsite to get to the bathroom or the dog park. Keeping the noise low is expected, even if it's outside quiet hours, so it's odd that the tenters have music playing. You'll rarely hear music in a campsite, rarely hear a television. You don't run your generator after quiet hours start—and light-noise counts, too, so turn off the bright outside lights. But the function of a campground is in that balance of community, the construction of community, and how we are alone together.

◼

MY MOTHER'S SIDE OF THE FAMILY SAVED EVERYTHING, from stacks of funeral bulletins to every single teaching contract my grandfather had, starting in 1948. The California side kept very little, though I've started to piece together some documentation. Most of what I have about my dad's family comes from my grandmother's sister, Katherine, up the English side of my grandmother's family. Years later, I would receive a box from my dad's cousin Sarah, Walt's youngest daughter, with Walt's war letters and some photographs, but that box in my stack of archival tubs is very small. Anything I've located of that side of the family has been in the intangible world of Ancestry.com and WikiTree, the scans of census records and birth records and naturalization records. I miss the tangibility of boxes of documents, the satisfaction of holding a piece of paper that meant something important enough to save it. I have baby hair curls, possible postmortem photographs, and ration cards for some branches—but none of that exists for the ancestral Babines. Nothing tangible to say *we were here, and this is the life we led.*

To go forward, we must go back. When Walt's first wife, Ada, died in 2018, Dad and I flew out to Santa Barbara for the funeral. Dad wanted to reconnect with his cousins, and I wanted to support my second cousin, Alana, daughter of Walt's youngest daughter. My dad hadn't seen or talked to any of them in decades. His cousin Sarah, Walt's youngest daughter, had spent a few years up in Kennebunk, Maine,

doing some research on the Babines, and over the course
of the last few years, she started passing on some of the archival documentation, photographs, letters, and ephemera
to me.

Walt's war letters to his mother smell so thickly of cig-
arette smoke that I need to air them out before I can read
them, before I can untie the stiff, dried-out green ribbon
used to tie them into bundles. I write my travel narratives
in a journal, but sometimes they exist as postcards or letters,
and the war letters in my family archives are a particular
kind of way we tell stories, or don't.

The first one, postmarked May 12, 1943, is addressed
to *Mr. and Mrs. Wm. Henry Babine*, on Walt's second day of
boot camp. He—and my grandfather—were only eighteen
years old.

There are no letters from July.

When the August letters begin, they are only addressed
to Mrs. Catherine Babine.

I feel the world slow as I realize the implications. Bill
Sr. died by suicide on July 28.

Oh, God.

This is the weight of the historian of futures past: holding those letters from May and June, I know things that
Walt does not. I know what's coming. And I just have to sit
there for a moment and let it pass.

In his early letters, Walt tells his mother that he misses
his dog, Rex, and wants her to bring him to visit on the days
when that's allowed. My father tells me he remembers Rex—
his bed was in the pantry. In a later letter from near the end
of the war, Walt laments the greenness of the eighteen-year-
olds joining them, how naive and untrained they are, and all
I can think is *you're only twenty*.

These letters are the only place Walt exists for me. He doesn't exist in stories or even photographs beyond 1943, even though he was alive until 1976. I have photographs of him with my grandfather as babies, as teenagers, a few from the war. His letters talk about wanting his mother to send him a camera, letting her know that he can't take photographs where he is—which he can't tell her—and *will send some snaps of myself soon*. I know what this boy who wrote these letters will become and I know what will happen to him thirty years from now.

But he does not know.

If I can say that Bill Sr. went to France, that he found himself in Flanders Fields, speaking the language of his bones in a place no Babine had seen for three hundred years, that he watched his fellow soldiers fall, that he faced the poison gas, that he watched his friends fall to the flu pandemic that killed twenty-five thousand from the American Expeditionary Force alone, that he came home to self-medicate his shell shock, I wonder if I can say that explains the ripple effects of what Alana once called *the shrapnel of family tragedy*.

It's a phrase I keep returning to: *the shrapnel of family tragedy*.

In 1943, Walt started out signing his letters *Walt* or *Walter*, but by the end of the war, he was signing them *Babe*. It took me longer than it should have to recognize the first syllable of our shared last name. The first day I started reading Walt's letters, I tried not to think about Catherine saving the letters from my grandfather and the likelihood that Marion threw them away. Marion was not sentimental in that way. By some miracle, there are four letters tucked into this pile addressed to my grandfather, and they certainly have a different tone than the ones sent to their mother. In several letters, Walt makes reference to my grandfather having woman trouble or spending time with "the femmes"—and the idea of my grandfather as a playboy is more than a little shocking, considering that's always been Walt's story, not my grandfather's. On September 8, 1944, Walt writes, *I got a letter from Bill enclosing the pictures of the chicks he went with at Lehigh. They sure are the cat's meow*—and then he veers hard into racist comments about the women around him. It seems the twins had a fairly decent relationship, with Walt writing to Catherine at some point that *Bill is a brother a fellow can be proud of* and wishing Bill would write more often.

I wonder what's been cut out by the censor, what the other side of the conversation—the letters my grandfather wrote to Walt—would say, what that would have revealed about their relationship, how competition for girls continued even so far apart, how the separation changed them, being apart for the first time in their lives, and what clues there might have been about the men they would grow into and how they would—or might have—internalized the death of their father, the war they both experienced in different ways influenced their adulthood and the families they made.

But here's what the letters don't say, never say. Maybe it's because he didn't want to worry his mother. Maybe Walt only wrote to his brother about being in combat, or being in a combat zone, since Bill had seen combat in Europe and could understand. I don't know. Absolutely nothing in Walt's saved letters alludes to combat, to the point where my father was a bit confused, because he'd always been under the impression that Walt had seen combat and PTSD was to blame for his violent behavior after he came home. On May 29, 1945, Walt writes, *Sometimes I get kinda mad just sitting around here.*

Been over 15 months and all I've done is sit around. When I go home, I'll just hang my head. In reading the letters, nobody would ever know he was in an active war zone. From the letters, it sounds like he was working a boring job and nothing interesting ever happened, but on September 8, 1944, he runs afoul of the censors and writes to his mother, *I've buzzed around a bit since I left the States. Have been [snipped]. Had a swell time at both places.* From later letters, I think this means Guadalcanal and Guam, or thereabouts. On April 2, 1945, it's the first letter in several weeks: *Dear Mom, I'll bet you thought I had forgotten you, but no, I hadn't. I've been moving again. We were 14 days abroad an [snipped] which explains why you didn't receive any mail from me.* He was transferred to the Sixth Marine Division in June 1945 and would have been at least adjacent to the Battle of Okinawa, which ended three days before he says his ship landed. His letter on July 17, 1945, reports: *Just got back from a quick trip to Okinawa and back. Very uneventful trip. Got a letter from both you and Bill today, the first mail I had received since the 18th of June, when I left to join this outfit. You can bet your life it was good to hear from you both. Bill never seems to put much news in his letters, maybe because there is none to write about, the same as it is here.*

I don't understand the "very uneventful trip," because the Battle of Okinawa was one of the bloodiest battles of the war, with nearly a quarter million casualties among the Japanese, Americans, and civilians. Even if the battle had ended by the time he got there, nothing about his work would have been uneventful. The Sixth Marine Division had been in the thick of it, so even if he didn't personally know people who had been on the ground, I wonder about just what Walt encountered when he arrived in the area. In the battle's aftermath, as reported in the *Marine Corps*

Gazette, troops were forced to leave dead friends behind, due to staggering casualty rates and poor weather, and "this, coupled with thousands of bodies both friend and foe littering the entire island, created a scent you could nearly taste." The *Gazette* records the incredible psychological toll this one battle left on the troops, and I wonder just what Walt saw—or smelled. Maybe there was nothing he could tell his mother, maybe he knew the censors would never let it through.

My dad reports that when he was in Guam in 1973 with the Air Force, the authorities had recently apprehended the last Japanese soldier on the island who had never surrendered. The story goes that the soldier, Shōichi Yokoi, had been told by his superior not to surrender until he returned, and then the superior officer never returned. After he was discovered, Yokoi said he had known the war was over since the 1950s, but he preferred death to the dishonor of capture and surrender.

For some, the war never ends.

For some, *le Grand Dérangement* persists, just one foot in front of another, yet never getting any further away. I smell it lingering in the smoke caught in the ribbon that binds these letters together, sharp in my nose.

AFTER BILL SR.'S DEATH, THE TWINS SET UP AN ALLOTMENT to send part of their military pay back to their mother, who, my father says, would have been working as an accountant at one of the local turkey hatcheries. I found the allotment application in Walt's service record at the National Archives annex.

She had a career, my father says, and I love this about her. The 1910 census—when she was nineteen—lists her as a bookkeeper at a drug store, and I wonder if she, her mother, and sister needed to get jobs after her father died in 1905 of tuberculosis at the age of forty-three. Her mother and sister worked in a corset factory, and I have a moment when I consider the multiple modes of restriction happening here. The stories my father has of his grandmother are stories of a strong woman who weathered her husband's suicide, the drafting of her boys, the emptiness of her house after they were gone to war. Dad says she wasn't afraid to shoot rattlesnakes in her yard with her .22—and hit them. She smoked Chesterfields like a chimney and made lemon meringue pie that was best described as *woody.*

From Walt's letters, it sounds like money was tight, and he and Grandpa sent home as much money as they could, I say.

They did, my father confirms. *But you know what? She didn't spend a dime of it. She banked it all and gave it back to them when they came home from the war.*

Then, in a box I've never seen before tucked into another box of things that came to me after my grandparents' deaths, a small stack of letters steals my breath.

April 7, 1976

Dear Bill and Marion—

It is so kind and thoughtful of you to invite me to go with you to Dan's wedding, and I'm really overwhelmed by the very thought of it. [. . .]

Everything here goes along much the same. David came down here last Wednesday 11pm. He is really mentally ill, filthy and dirty. He went back Friday to get his clothes, and belongings and we will have him stay here, and try to straighten him out, if we can. When you see him, you can feel that all your worries are trivial and thank God that you do not have that burden to bear. I am sorry this letter is not more cheerful, but I am being honest, and facing the truth as I see it. I am praying for him, and for all, and trust that God will show us the way.

Love to all,
Mother

I read on, hearing the click of a minute hand in my head. The family would have been deep in planning to travel for my parents' wedding. I hold the letter carefully, hardly breathing, as if I'll disturb something that should be left alone, and I recognize the same kind of stillness I felt in my father's office, the day I asked why Catherine and Walt shared a death date. The moment, somehow, felt predatory. I wonder what Catherine's body knew about David that her mind did not.

April 29, 1976

Dear Bill and Marion—

I wish that I felt able to make the trip, but I'm afraid I would be ill again, and spoil everything for you. If I tried to go it would be against my better judgment, and it is indeed very tempting to think about it anyway.

David is here, and seems to have calmed down, and feeling better. He has been working making jewelry, and really stays with it. I hope we will be able to help him get going.

Love to all,
Mother

Three days after this letter, she and Walt were dead. Everything in my mind goes quiet, and this fragment slides up against a moment from another place, another time: when Walt's first wife, Ada, died in 2018, at dinner after her funeral, conversation naturally turned to her children who were not present.

Around the table, a friend of their family whose name I never caught said, *I saw David the day he did it.* She paused. *And he just smelled wrong.*

This is why history—and family history—matters, because it's always new context, the placing of feet on a particular moment so that we can understand how data becomes knowledge. Nothing in any of the data would have given me *he just smelled wrong*, and that's the moment everything hinges on. History isn't a melody line—it's a chord. It's always the accumulation of moments that don't seem to have meaning in themselves adding up to a moment that tells us everything. It's a long game, this kind of faith, because there's no destination. It's a circle, a circuit, or a labyrinth. And it exists outside of time. I think about this moment a lot, the ephemeral nature of what we know and how we know it, whether it's written into paper and preserved or lodged in our sensory memories, what our bodies know, how we pass down what's important enough about survival to be written onto paper or into our instincts. *He just smelled wrong.* She said that when she heard about the murders later, she was shocked but not surprised.

And I think about timelines of history, that I can hold this fragile paper in my hand and recognize how much I know that my great-grandmother did not, and how it feels like a responsibility to bear the right kind of witness.

As I get closer to Acadie, I return to my constant wondering about events becoming history when we no longer carry them in our bodies. This woman who knew *David just smelled wrong* carried in her body some kind of evolutionary knowledge of danger. I wonder what instinct Grandpa and Walt developed in their own theaters of war, for the smell of cordite or the humid heat of decay or the particular pitch of a bell, and I wonder about what happens when the woman with the knowledge of David in her bones will be gone, and I will be left with the documents, the archive of Catherine's death certificate, and the injuries listed under cause of death, Walt's letters permeated with smoke.

CHAPTER EIGHT

QUEBEC CITY IS A TRULY BEAUTIFUL PLACE, THE KIND of beauty valued by my northern European ancestors who wanted this specific combination of blue and green in their homelands as well as those places they chose to immigrate to. I know these trees, the birch and the pine, the shapes of their leaves, the spikes of their needles. Had someone passed me a photograph of this place and asked me to identify it, I would have placed it somewhere on the Minnesotan North Shore of Lake Superior, maybe even Copper Harbor in Michigan, the Canadian Shield of granite that forms my own bedrock as well as the bedrock of Quebec.

This familiar granite, while some of the oldest exposed rock formation on the planet, is literally shaped like a shield, starting in the far north-central of the Northwest Territories, cutting a swath through the middle of Manitoba, the southern two-thirds of Ontario and down a bit into Minnesota, and up again to encompass all of Quebec. The shield is a shape that protects—but what it protects and what or whom it protects from give me pause. The soil here is very thin, and much of this skin of rock is visible, an igneous reminder that once burned its volcanic history into these shapes. In this place, I can touch the skeleton of the planet and wonder about the shape it gives to the stories told on it.

———

IN THE NOT-SO-DISTANT PAST: A MAN NAMED PATRICK sat on his collapsible stool on the breakwater at Berthier-sur-Mer, just north of Quebec City, the St. Lawrence River a gritty shade of blue in the oppressive July morning. The shards of notes from his uilleann pipes cut through the humidity, vibrato in the layered strands that pull like taffy, the bass notes a dull heat in my bones and the stones of the mountains that line the shore of the river, the melody rippling the heavy air in front of us. The tune was medium tempo, cheerful, and it made us restless as we waited for the ferry that would take us to Grosse Île, into a history I only knew intellectually, a history that does not belong to my blood, but a history I was curious about anyway. What I did not know at the time is that this moment, this place, would become valuable two years in the future, the slide of history stretching and condensing. Whatever expression masked Patrick's face, it was not the same elemental joy I had seen a few nights before on the face of Gearóid Ó hAllmhuráin, with his uilleann pipes that were older than the chapel we were sitting in, playing with champion fiddler Pierre Schryer. This morning, here, Patrick's face wore the granite of the Canadian Shield as his skin.

ILL-un. Uilleann pipes, the Irish bagpipe. It's a word I did not know, an instrument I didn't know, in two languages I didn't know. In the heart of Quebec, the Irish music I had been hearing for the last few days had blended so completely with the traditional Quebecois music that I didn't know where one ended and the other began. Two nights ago, listening to Gearóid and Pierre, the planks of the chapel floor had vibrated beneath my feet as a hundred other people tapped along to their tunes, that unconscious and unexpected quality of music made physical. This morning, listening to Patrick, there was something about these pipes that raised goosebumps on my arms in the heat and an anticipation of something I knew was coming, though I did not know what form it would take. My body knew something that my head did not yet know.

During the summer of 1847, a hundred thousand Irish immigrants crowded this river, the tall masts of the ships that carried them interrupting the horizon, this island, more than three times the number of immigrants the station had ever seen in a year. As we chugged closer on our ferry, I tried to imagine the sheer noise of the river as it might have been in 1847, the creaking ships, the snap of sails, the voices carrying so clearly across water, and I wondered about the smells—of bodies, sickness, death. We disembarked with jackets over our arms, umbrellas dangling from our wrists, because we had been warned that it can get cool on Grosse Île, but we laughed as we raised our umbrellas against the heat of this incredible sun. I wrapped myself in the physical senses of those tall-masted ships in my imagination, the sheer noise of the creaking wood of the hulls across the flat plane of that water, the snap of sails, the burning sensation of hope into grief, like sunburn. We passed an immense warehouse on the wharf, built in 1892, that we would find out later was the shed used for disinfecting not only immigrants but the immigrants' belongings also. At the time it was constructed, it was the height of medical ingenuity. Inside, I could not shake images of the Holocaust in the showers, the steam ovens.

Because this island was a graveyard.

And yet this was not a landscape of loss; the story of Grosse Île, while a narrative of grief, is something else entirely. The grief it represented was an adding to, not a taking away, not the same way that the empty places in Ireland where these immigrants came from are a landscape of loss. I did not understand yet what it *was*, but I knew what it was not.

We met our tour guide in the shade of the third-class hotel, and he told us that his name was Pierre-Loup. His voice had the unique cadence of the Maritimes that I originally took for the inflection of one who has spent time in Ireland. What I would not know for several more years was that the accent in parts of the Canadian Maritimes sounds very Irish.

He told us Grosse Île was never an immigration station like Ellis Island; its only purpose was to prevent immigrants from bringing illnesses into Canada that could become epidemics, preventing a repeat of the 1832 cholera epidemic. Pierre-Loup told us how many immigrants crossed through Grosse Île in its early years: usually between twenty thousand and thirty thousand, two-thirds of whom were Irish, traveling on ships not meant for human habitation, sailing ships that took six weeks to cross the Atlantic. Add in the poor health of those starving immigrants and medical theory of miasma, which understood little of how diseases spread or their incubation periods, and the death rates of those headed toward Grosse Île were fairly high. It was the summer of 1847 that had the most impact on the physical and emotional shape of this island, a six-month period that would separate its bedrock into a clear Before and After.

Pierre-Loup spoke of those *buried* on Grosse Île, not those who *died* here, because he told us that once ships entered the St. Lawrence, they were no longer allowed to conduct burials at sea, because officials were worried that the tides would carry those bodies down the river to Quebec City and Montreal, so the dead were simply stored until the ships arrived at their destinations. Some who left the island after quarantine were still infected with cholera or typhus and died elsewhere, in some cases spreading the disease they were quarantined against. I know some of my own Irish ancestors left under these circumstances on their way to Boston, but I have not yet spent much time inside that line of the family tree. Later I would think of migration, forced migration, landscapes of movement, how the Famine forced a million Irish from their land as another million starved, only to come to the place my Acadian ancestors had been forcibly removed from less than a hundred years before. I would wonder what the British thought of the Irish Catholics inhabiting the space created by the expulsion of French Catholics. History inflates like an accordion, or a concertina, pulling apart, condensing, and I think I can hear its music.

There are seven thousand five hundred and fifty-three people buried on this little island, Pierre-Loup told us, his accent clipping the *h*'s in *t'ousand* and *t'ree*. Of those seven thousand five hundred and fifty three—a number that must be laid down in words, not numerical symbols—five thousand four hundred and twenty-four of them were Irish, Irish who died in that six-month period during that summer of

1847, accounting for more than three-quarters of all those buried on this island.

This is intellectual knowledge, not knowledge in your bones. There's a difference.

The bones on this island represented a knowledge I was not sure I was ready for.

———

WE FOLLOWED PIERRE-LOUP DOWN THE CRUSHED-ROCK path toward an expanse of grass bounded by a picket fence, the vertical struts of white an unexpected break in that horizontal green. As we neared, we could see irregularly placed white wooden crosses, large, almost clumsy in their construction and placement. At the apex of the hill, we could fix the entire expanse in our field of vision, but what we were seeing was still not clear. This meadow-cemetery, about the size of a football field, is the mass grave for nearly all of the 5,424 Irish who died during that summer of 1847, but it didn't look like a cemetery should look. Without the crosses, I would never have known. The land flowed in wide ripples, rising and falling into rows and deep troughs. This was not a smooth expanse of land, of grass, of memory.

I had assumed that those 5,424 people were buried on the raised portions of the cemetery, assumed that since there were so many of them dying in such a short period of time that they would have just been piled on top of each other and covered with dirt, a visual reference to various mass graves I had seen on the news over the course of my life. But it wasn't like that. *Everyone who was buried on the island,* Pierre-Loup said, *was treated with respect, and every single one of them not only got a coffin but they got their own coffin.* What

I was looking at here were coffins, buried three deep, one on top of another, but I was looking in the wrong place. When the bodies and the coffins began to decompose, the earth above them collapsed, so if I were looking for the specter of those 5,424 people, I would find them in the spaces where the land dipped, kept nearly in shadow except at high noon when the sun was directly overhead.

That was what froze my mind in place, a place I would return to when walking the churchyards in Yarmouth and Ste. Anne du Ruisseau and the graveyards at the Fort Anne Historic Site in Port-Royal and elsewhere in search of the Babines buried there. Grosse Île is the place that taught me the meaning of this particular landshape, how to listen to it, and this remains one of the most important modes of understanding the ways history is recorded—the way it is told and in what language—that I have ever encountered. Because my memory is spatial, I cannot separate this moment, this heat, and this shock of understanding from the view in my mind.

In this space of heat shimmers, Patrick again set up his stool, this time behind us, and at a motion from our host, he began a lament on those uilleann pipes, putting the topography in front of us into the rise and fall of his notes, like waves against the shoreline of this island, a rippling kind of sound, that solid droning bass note so low it was felt more than heard. After the moment of silence that followed the last notes, a woman named Margaret read a poem by an Irish Canadian author, and I think we all stopped breathing. Certainly nobody moved. When she finished, we stayed still and silent as Patrick picked up his low whistle and began to play again. In time, some of us moved to the memorial wall that bore the inscribed names of the dead, the stone memorial carved with the names of the physicians who died that summer after being infected by their patients. We eventually returned within earshot of Patrick, let him do our grieving for us.

This is a place that resists narrative, resists story, takes the human desire to understand the shape of the history in front of us and upends it, asks the essential questions of *at what point does individual history become part of the collective?* and *where is the opposite true?* Even more specifically, Grosse Île is a place that causes us to ask what we do with the question at all. Is it even answerable?

We then climbed the hill to the cliff where the Irish memorial cross stood sentry. Some, still visibly shaken from the visit to the Irish cemetery, stood in the shade while others peered closer. We were nearing the noon hour, and the heat was becoming dangerous, more than simply unbearable. We kept looking to the sky, hoping for the thunderstorm that had been promised for that afternoon, yet the sky still bore that flattened blue color. The air was deadly thick and still. We were feeling the oppression that was Grosse Île on this particular day, the stone and the water, the sun and humidity, the weight of what we were seeing and not seeing. This place had memory, and it was holding that memory in a fist.

Then, a moment so surreal that it could have been invented but was not. Picture this: a crowd of twenty people, ranging in age from midtwenties to mideighties, standing around a fifty-foot-tall Celtic cross, physically uncomfortable, psychically uncomfortable, wishing for so many reasons not to be here in this place right now. We were listening to the lilt and gutter of the Irish language, most of us with closed eyes, and at the exact moment the woman finished reading the plaque's Irish translation, the wind came up, blew our umbrellas inside out, and whipped our hair into our faces, and we stumbled to stand straight in an environment that had suddenly matched its exterior to our interiors. I wish I could say that the thunderstorm broke at that point, clouds tossing lightning bolts and rolling thunder down the horizontal plane of the river, but that did not happen. The humidity did not break, the heat did not break, and neither did we. The only change was that wind, and we quickly moved away from the cliff edge, because it was enough to blow us over if we found ourselves too close. This was the only spot of emotional importance on Grosse Île where Patrick did not play that day, and I wonder what he would have chosen, the low whistle or the uilleann pipes, the tone and the tenor, the tempo and the tune.

Speech was impossible on the descent to the first-class hotel, but even if we had words, the wind was too loud to hear each other, that incomprehensible clash of air and moisture in the upper atmosphere. I offered my arm to a very tiny, slight octogenarian with white hair permed so tightly that her curls did not budge in the wind. Inside the first-class hotel, over our lunch of sandwiches, when we were able to find some relief from the wind, we quietly commented to each other about how loud the wind was, but *loud* wasn't quite the right word—it was the pressure it had exerted on our ears without any sort of sound.

＊

Two years later, when I cross by Grosse Île en route to a different path of history, I wonder how many ways stories can be recorded—and told—without words, only pulled into being by holding presence in a moment that matters.

135

CHAPTER NINE

I LEAVE QUEBEC CITY AND ITS ECHOES OF GROSSE ÎLE behind in the early morning, and so my arrival to Fundy National Park is much earlier than I anticipate. I'm starting to feel like my experience on that little island two years ago set me up for the Bay of Fundy now in ways I could not have understood at the time. My mind and memory are full of the stories that landshapes tell, how the stories remain in the land even when there are no voices left. History and time are sliding against each other again, in a way that makes me feel like I need to accumulate thoughts, collect experiences, pay particular and specific attention to what's around me, because I don't know when, in the course of my own history, it may become important.

Fundy National Park has a good campground, full of trees and light and bird noise, and it's nearly empty of other campers. Once I'm set up, Galway heads under the bedspread, as per usual, Maeve further down the bed, where she can see out the window and warn of approaching birds and squirrels. I watch both of them settle while I eat my peanut butter and honey sandwich at the dinette table, and I'm fairly sure I can hear Galway's mental screaming that *there's too much nature out there!* and Maeve's determination to murder every small creature within range. Then I pack up the Jeep with water and snacks and go in search of the Bay of Fundy via the little town of Alma, where I will fill up the gas tank.

I have the whole day to play and I'm pretty excited about it. I'm so tired of driving and driving so hard. It feels like a gift to have finally reached the Bay of Fundy, where I expect Great Sights and Great Thoughts and Great Stories. I walk around the beach in Alma for a while—the tide is out, and it's nice to stretch a little after being in the car for so long, just breathe air that doesn't feel canned and recycled. After that, I go to the visitor's center. But the light feels flat somehow, the day without dimension, and I don't know what to make of it. I should do things, think things, feel things, connect things. To my irritation, nothing is clicking. I hike to see Dickson Falls—not far—and then drive through a covered bridge en route to Point Wolfe, but the colors of the day feel washed out, and I don't know why. I want to get down to the beach there, but I can't figure out how, and my excitement over the day seems to slide away. I'm supposed to be making memories, for crying out loud, and the day is actively working against that. The frustration mounts, builds in my spine, in my breath.

I am not in a mood to wander, so the walking is less than satisfying, and the relative difficulty in figuring out how to get from where I am to where I want to go isn't inspiring me to put much more brain power to it, and my lack of connection or interesting thoughts or anything else becomes more irritating as the afternoon stretches. It feels like I'm collecting an experience simply for the object of it, not out of any curiosity or any moment of exploration.

Maybe it's because my brain is not in a place to be still, to be curious, and I just can't recognize it at the time. There's a difference between spontaneous experiences, those you put yourself in the path of because you figure something will happen, like Grosse Île, and the places that elude you entirely. This will become one of them.

Later, I'll think about resonance, waves, frequencies, what we can hear, what we can't hear, what the natural world knows that the human body cannot comprehend, the tides in the Bay of Fundy, the tidal resonance that's unique to the shape of this place, the shape of the wave action that makes the water more powerful here than other places. I think about the first Tacoma Narrows Bridge, "Galloping Gertie," which, due to a mistake in engineering, was uniquely capable of catching the wind at the right frequency to achieve harmonic resonance, which made the bridge vibrate. In 1940, in a miraculous moment caught on video, the bridge bucked and waved and pulled like taffy and broke apart and fell into the river. I keep thinking about Castleton Tower in Utah, vibrating at the same pitch as the human heart, as I did a few days ago at Kakabeka Falls, wondering about the pitch of the water that felt so good to me. Alma, Point Wolfe—they didn't resonate for me. I don't know why, even as I wish they did.

There's a lot of pressure on travel; I want to collect all these Meaningful Experiences to add stories to my repertoire of A Life Well Lived™, telling myself that everything can be An Experience if I approach it with the right frame of mind. After all, who knows if I'll ever get back to Dublin again, or London, or San Francisco? If I never come back to the Maritimes, what do I want to take home that will last me forever? If I never come back to Nova Scotia, what do I want to make sure comes home with me? Rocks from the Bay of Fundy, new family data and photos of gravestones, some deeper understanding of how this family removed storytelling from who it was as a family? It's taken a while to break myself of that souvenir mindset. Sometimes I've done it literally: lately, any souvenirs I've bought have been tea or other things meant to be consumed, not meant to sit on a shelf and collect dust. My dad's grandmother bought a teacup whenever she traveled, amassing an eclectic collection that was passed down to my sisters and me because nobody else wanted them, a moment when the teacups themselves were the only record of her travels because dementia had stolen her memories. I don't carry the memories that made these cups important to her, but it's enough to know that I can create new memories with them. Years later, my dad will go online to buy me tea from the little shop in Mahone Bay and give it to me for Christmas, memories of the Atlantic side of Nova Scotia fragrant in my cup, and the memory-flavor of the place will pull itself up from the past into the present.

On family camping trips, our parents bought us one souvenir T-shirt for the trip. We could get it anywhere we wanted, but we only got one, so we had to make a good choice. The one thing we were given an unlimited supply of was film, which was likely as expensive for frugal parents as several T-shirts would have been, and this was the basis for the digital Scamp Camera I bought for the kids to use when they camped with me—they could take as many pictures as they wanted. On my first non-family trip, to Mexico during my junior year of high school with my Spanish class, I brought home indiscriminate souvenirs for family, without much thought to how the people I bought them for might like or not like them. I thought they should love them simply because I thought of them when I bought it. Of course, this is not the way it works, and I always felt a little sad that they didn't value the souvenirs in the way I did, but why would they, when the earrings or the clothes didn't carry the same memories and emotional weight for them?

Rocks have been my preferred souvenir for years and they're definitely not a souvenir that transfers meaning well. *When do kids pick up their fascination with rocks—and why?* Certainly, mine started early and has never gone away, and there's a reason I spent several hours at the Amethyst Mine Panorama in Thunder Bay, mildly mindful of the woman at the front desk who told me to be careful, that amethyst can cut like glass, as I started sifting through the rocks between my knees. The ground was just *purple*, and I couldn't get over the novelty of it. I sorted by color first, then shape, realizing that I really like the chunks that were at least two colors. Some were clumps of crystals, some reminded me of teeth. I made piles to give to Cora and Henry, even though he was only eighteen months old at the time. The rest were just for me, because I've clearly not outgrown the need to add to my own rock collection, and I became glad, not for the last time on this trip, that I'm driving and can pack as much rock in the back of my Jeep as I have space for.

When Cora is nine, we will hunt for pretty stones for Mancala and play it in my parents' camper as Lake Superior rages around us. The weather is not good, and I'm deep in the grief of our first camping trip without Mom, but I am not physically capable of saying no when Cora asks if we can go down to the beach and look for agates. It's just what you do when you come to Lake Superior: you look for agates. I know it will take me several hours to warm up once I'm cold, but we've already nixed a campfire because it's raining, and to keep saying no to this kid is not a thing I can do. My Jeep is in the shop, so we're not Scamping, and Dad offered to be our third, and so the three of us set up camp in his fifth wheel.

When I was growing up, Dad rarely played games with us—still doesn't—but when Cora and I wash up our new Mancala stones and decide which twenty-four are the best of the bunch and settled down to play at the table, I ask Dad if he wants to play the winner, and he doesn't even hesitate to jump in. He and Cora play rock paper scissors to decide who goes first. Mancala becomes a permanent part of our camping-together experiences, as it's a game we can play and not get tired of, and the smallest kids can play without trouble, and I will continue to collect stones from various places—like Petoskey and Charlevoix stones from Michigan—to make the game more memorable. We'll hold the stories of the planet in our hands and use them to make new stories and consider ways of understanding what is tangible and physical memory, that history is alive, that geology is alive, in motion, that it's always in present tense, even if the rock is billions of years old. In the spring thaw, we still see the stories of the last ice age pushed to the surface, stories that had been buried for thousands of years.

━━━

WHEN I GET BACK TO MY CAMPSITE, I TRY TO START A FIRE for coals for dinner, but the wood is green, again. The sun is bright and beautiful, the sky blue and cheerful, and it is pure pleasure just to putter around the campsite, to read in my chair while the fire sputters and smokes, glad that the campground is empty enough that I don't have to be actively ashamed of my fire. After two hours of deep and embarrassing pyromaniac failure, I pull out the induction cooktop, and in a short amount of time, I'm frying up leftovers and grilling up the asparagus I'd picked up near Quebec City.

Then the black flies descend, and there is no relief or escape.

I retreat to the Scamp in defeat.

Some days are like that.

———

IN MY HOUSE, 57 DEGREES MEANS SOMETHING HAS GONE terribly wrong. In the camper, 57 degrees feels like a gift. This is a morning like that, just on the edge of too chilly to want to get out of bed, of wanting to stay snuggled up with the electric blanket and the cats. It's easier to stay warm than it is to get warm in the first place. I want to head to see the Hopewell Rocks, but there's no good reason to hurry. They haven't moved much in a few million years. Soon enough, the call of the teapot is enough to pull me out of the cocoon, locate the thick socks, and start the electric kettle. Galway is under the topmost blanket, as usual, and Maeve is stretched out along the foot of the bed. It's quiet, and chilly, and the most perfect kind of camping morning there is.

Mornings like this, I wonder about people who camp full-time, and people who live full-time in Scamps, either the thirteen-foot like mine or the sixteen-foot. My Scamp is my escape pod, both logistically and emotionally, and sometimes I wonder what it would be like to live in it permanently, or at least long-term enough that it's real life, not a trip. Certainly, this trip is long enough that I'm getting a taste of it. The reality is you cannot transfer your grounded life into the Scamp life. You're not downsizing, having the whole life smaller and more portable. You have to recognize it's a whole different life. It's not about lessening your load—it's about picking up another load entirely. Fulltiming in the Scamp would be an intentional shift in values, because things that are valuable at home are not valuable on the road—which seems obvious when I say it out loud, but the value part is important. I might source all my clothes, professional and otherwise, from thrift stores, but the values that I carry around in those clothes don't transfer in the same way to the Scamp. I don't really care that I have worn pretty much the same tank top and jeans for a couple of days, as long as they're not dirty or smelly. At home, I dry everything on drying racks to save on electricity. When I camp, everything has to be able to go in the dryer.

In the Scamp, what I value shifts from levels of cleanliness to efficiency of effort. Showers become less important than the small act of becoming clean, because the work of showering is such a process, and your dreams of a hot shower are often tempered by the reality of Navy showers, needlelike sprays, and subpar cleanliness standards. Beyond gathering up your dopp kit and your towel, you need shower shoes, because nobody needs whatever is growing in those showers. The Shower Dress is one of the best ideas I've come across in recent years, just any easy cotton dress to wear to and from the shower house, because trying to wrestle on clean clothes when you're only half-dry in a small shower space—where there may or may not be a bench so you have to do your best one-legged flamingo without tipping over and crashing into the wall and embarrassing yourself further—is to be avoided if possible. So, the Shower Dress.

Still, given all the effort of showering and hair drying, I really, really have to want it.

Everything about Scamp life is about efficacy, and efficiency of effort. How can I justify the energy expended in this task? What's necessary, what's not necessary? At home I'm a cook, but when I'm on the road, I'm not. I can't even replicate how I eat at home with how I eat on the road—and it's a good reminder that home life doesn't translate easily to Scamp life, which is not the same as Scamp travel. I eat differently in the Scamp than I do at home because I can't keep as much fresh food in the camper. When I'm Scamping, I like instant oatmeal with freeze-dried fruit, or hard-boiled eggs from Costco. At home, I'll cook up soup and freeze it for lunches, but I can't do that in the Scamp, so I eat peanut butter sandwiches with either honey or jam. Honey doesn't need refrigeration. I'm vegetarian, so most fast food is out for me. It's easier to store bread than it is to store other things, but when I'm on the road, I often forget to stop for lunch; it's 1:00 or 2:00 p.m., and I haven't eaten, and I should, and then I wonder why I get to my campsite with a migraine. Somehow, I do not learn from this knowledge.

Just like that first trip to Ireland with the pack I couldn't lift by myself, we learn what we're capable of carrying on our own, because we can't depend on anyone else to do it for us. If I don't do it, it doesn't get done. These days, particularly now that I've reached New Brunswick and there are things here I'm excited to see, I know there's going to be a lot of accumulation. In the moment, I'm not going to know what's going to be important and what I can let the tides take away.

I PACK UP MY CAMERA AND HEAD TOWARD HOPEWELL Rocks, and the sun comes out about half an hour into the drive. Waiting a bit was a good choice. I pay my admission and walk down the steps built into the cliff to see the Flowerpots, which are best experienced from the seabed unveiled at low tide. The construction of the steps, made of grate and heavily tractioned, makes it clear that the tide and wave action is dramatic enough to rise that high. It is impressive, even before I see the Flowerpots.

The tide is out, and I'm reminded what a marvel is geologic time, stories written into the earth. Were my Babin ancestors ever in this area, what they would have seen several hundred years ago would not be much different than what I see now, eroded sea stacks forty to seventy feet tall, narrower around the bases, some with trees and vegetation growing on the tops, and I absolutely do not care that my reactions are deeply clichéd, because this is a wondrous place. There are seventeen sea stacks here, some with fanciful names like Elephant Rock. Whatever meaningful experience I did not have yesterday, I've found it today. This is just plain delightful.

At high tide, all but the tops of the rocks are hidden below the water. It's an impressive sight, just the visual drama of nothing and something. It's here that I learn the reality of tides, that what I'm seeing—or not seeing—is one of the four ways that water moves in this place. What's here are vertical tides, the empty bay floor, the metal steps that disappear when the tide rises. The horizontal tide, the distance between how far out the water needs to travel to fill the flats, I'll understand that better at Blue Beach in Nova Scotia in a few days.

We're warned by prominent signs not to go into the mudflats.

And yet, a group of four college-age boys are exploring the mudflats in front of me, and they've decided to take off their shoes and walk in the mud.

It's like walking through pudding! one of them exclaims.

A young father and a young son, both mudded up to their calves, rejoin a young woman, and she looks at them and says, *Well, I hope Daddy has a good plan to clean you two up!*

Dad laughs and says, *Yeah, I didn't think that far ahead.*

Maybe, just as we never outgrow our rock collecting loves, we never quite outgrow the joy of mud either.

Sometimes I wonder about the compulsion of going in search of family history, something I encounter often when encountering Americans traveling in Ireland, and sometimes I wonder why we want to find the records and graves of people who lived and died a hundred years ago, people we've never met, people who have no bearing on who we are right now. Of course, we never find *them*—at best, we find a grave, bones to dust, a name scratched into a church register as some kind of tangible proof they existed, that we didn't spring into existence from nothing. We can't know it, of course, we can't know their likes and dislikes and allergies and hobbies and skills and the things they were absolutely hopeless at, so it's curious to me that the quest for historical tangibles remains a part of so many families, including mine.

Being the family historian is not much different than a form of ancestor worship, and that connection to ancestors is something I can understand, especially as the niblings will get older and attend a Spanish immersion school, and the Day of the Dead will become a part of our very, very northern European family's rituals. My mother passes away on All Saint's Day, and because the kids watched *Coco* at school only a day or two before, explaining Nana's death to them is much easier. Each year, the *ofrenda* becomes more elaborate, and it's deeply comforting; even though it's not a cultural tradition we grew up with, it becomes part of the way we construct the bridges between family, past and present, alive and gone. Then we set up the family viewing of *Coco* so that we can all watch together, wherever we are, geographically.

It's not a matter of locating the ancestors—they're not lost. My mother is not lost; neither are the Babines I've come to Nova Scotia to find. The ancestors are not the Flowerpots, which are only visible in their entirety when the tides retreat. And yet, there's something nearly universal in *wanting, needing* to be connected to the ancestors, to my mother and my brother-in-law Mike's father, who are gone, or our grandparents, whether it's filial piety, or ancestor veneration, or the Day of the Dead, or communion with microfilm. Why do many of us carry this need to belong to an established history? What happens when that can't—or shouldn't—happen? When is our individual history more valuable than the communal history we're connected to, like my grandfather seemed to believe? Over the years, I've read accounts of well-meaning teachers assigning family tree projects to students, which assumes a traditional and intact family structure, but doesn't take into account divorce, foster care, adoption, infidelity, violence, family that is not worth having, secrets that are not for sharing. It forces conversations that families are not ready to have— *why do Catherine and Walt have the same death date?*—and absolutely ignores the residual trauma of Black students whose ancestral records won't go past 1865, or Native children who face removal from their parents at significantly higher rates than non-Native children and the historical

trauma of boarding schools that aimed to forcibly assimi-
late Native children in ways that still reverberate today. In
my home state of Minnesota, according to the National
Indian Child Welfare Organization (NICWA), Native
children make up 1.7 percent of the population, but represent 25.8 percent of children in foster care. The rest of the
Midwest has similar numbers as compared to other regions
of the United States. This kind of work is not neutral.

*What is revealed and what is hidden as those ancestral tides
come and go?*

There's damage to be done in the quest for Family™.
We see the damage when legislation is enacted to prevent
LGBTQ couples from adopting, when religious organiza-
tions are permitted to deny services in the name of *family*.
We hear about politicians pushing anti-women legislation
that keeps us from abortion, contraceptives, and other health
care, the death of Savita Halappanavar in Ireland and the rise
of these stories in the United States in a post-Roe world, and
then those same politicians cutting social welfare programs
that would allow women to create and support the children
those politicians seem so desperately to want them to produce. And yet, we're still conditioned not to get angry over
the children impregnated by fathers and uncles, about rape
victims not only forced to carry the fetus to term but forced to
share custody with their rapist. It's difficult not to internalize
this as a young woman and decide that this is not a safe place
to create children, even if I had the inclination. Now we hear
complaints about declining birth rates, how my generation
can't afford to have children, and how anti-abortion legislation is designed to create babies for the adoption industry.
When a sixteen-year-old orphan in Florida is deemed by the
courts to be too immature to make the decision to terminate

her pregnancy but not immature enough to bear that child, the goal to convince her to put that child up for adoption becomes blindingly and predatorily transparent.

We hear too many stories of family arguing that *family does anything for family*, that *blood is thicker than water*, when the act of forcing somebody to house a toxic family member or bail them out or even simply allow them to attend family functions is deeply damaging. How does a family, found or otherwise, create a shell to protect itself not just from the major trauma of war, or murder, or suicide and its effect on a family, but also the microtraumas of disinterest and distance? In her book, *Micro-trauma: A Psychoanalytic Understanding of Cumulative Psychic Injury*, Margaret Crastnopol observes that

> *injurious relating on the grossly abusive end of the scale is the time-honored stuff of history, fiction, drama, and contemporary psychoanalytic theory. But negative interactions that are evanescent can ultimately also have a strong psychic impact. Like sharp rocks only vaguely if at all visible beneath the water at the shore, such potentially damaging moments may go largely unregistered. As a result, these subtler occurrences, especially in the aggregate, can create psychic bruises that are hard to notice and harder to minister to, with the consequence that they accumulate invisibly. Such injuries can distort a person's character, undermine his or her sense of self-worth, and compromise his or her relatedness to others.*

Small things, over time, accumulate in ways that echo. How do family members pass down what they know so that future generations will not make the same mistakes, will be safe, will not be affected by the same hurt?

I don't know.

Over the years, as my niblings arrive, I will need to deliberately create my place in the family, because there is no societal default for a solo person who doesn't want kids, one who lives far away from the day-to-day life of the family. I've always had a clear place in the family as an aunt—and it's worth mentioning that the kids only have unmarried aunts without kids—but because of the physical distance between us, I've had to be more deliberate about who I want to be when I'm with them. I won't give the kids cousins to play with, but I will give them cats, whose presence seems to always be more exciting than mine. Kim's the aunt who will play Legos with them; I'm the one who's going to take them camping. I will model my aunting identity on Marion's sister, Great-Aunt Katherine (and Uncle Dick), and Aunt Teresa (and Uncle Robin), the only California family who always seemed excited to see us when we visited.

Once I start camping with the kids, I come to appreciate what I call Practical Scamping: taking my home with me, parking it in somebody's driveway, and sleeping in my own bed, like the California Grandparents did when they came to visit. I have to admit they were onto something with the whole idea.

One day, just a few years back now, I'll come to visit my family and park the Scamp in the driveway, because it's easier to sleep in my own bed and manage Galway—who is elderly, blind, toothless, and now solo, with Maeve having gone suddenly the year before—away from three active niblings and two active dogs. On the first morning, I'll awake to a persistent tapping on the outside of the camper. I look at the clock: 6:06 a.m. The noise continues. I move the curtain enough to see a tiny blond head at the door, the garage door open.

I open the door to my four-year-old nephew Sam, bouncing with excitement that I think is deeply unreasonable at 6:06 a.m.

How is Galway? he chitters.

I stare at him blankly, consciousness not scheduled to arrive for another hour. *Are you okay? Is anybody else up? Do they know you're here?*

Sam laughs in the bright way of small children in wee hours, ignores the questions, and crawls up on the bed to see the cat, who is not thrilled to see him. I squint at the clock again and try to convince myself that I don't care that Sam has come out at the crack of dawn to see the cat, not me, his aunt.

How did you get the garage door open?

I used Cora's boot, he says matter-of-factly as he runs his hand down Galway's back, ignoring the cat's baleful expression.

Of course he did. The child is a very short evil genius.

I'm not going back to sleep while he is the only one awake in the house, so I reach for my clothes. *Do you want some breakfast?*

Yes, he says decisively, still stroking Galway. *Yogurt.*

Off we go to find ourselves some yogurt and a lot of caffeine, over which I'll learn all about the breakfast preferences of various dinosaurs, and apparently they all like yogurt. Which kind of yogurt depends on species, but granola is not negotiable, I'm told. All dinosaurs like granola. One must not mix up dinosaurs and dragons, because they have entirely different dietary needs and palates.

I tell Sam he can come out to visit me again only if there's an adult in the house awake enough to know where he is. He nods.

But right now, as I am on the road to Acadie, Sam is still two years away from joining the tale at all, let alone coordinated enough to use his sister's boot to tap the garage door opener so he can visit my cat, and several years further still from the first time I'll take him to Duluth with me. I wonder what he'll think of Glensheen. I expect Cora, when she joins me at age seven, to absolutely love it, but she'll follow the tour guide like she is faintly afraid of him, of the house, of the weight of memory. She will find her enthusiasm for the place and what she's seen later that afternoon when we're painting story stones on the picnic table next to the Scamp, like she's had to think her way through it, sift through memories and impressions like flip cards, before she can articulate herself.

CHAPTER TEN

I LEAVE FUNDY NATIONAL PARK AND ITS UNREASONABLE infestation of black flies under clear skies and brave the grade down to Alma, where the tide is out. I don't get lost on my way to Moncton, which is unexpected, but when I get there, the mood inside the Atlantic Superstore where I stop to buy more silverware is silent in a way I don't understand. I go looking for tortillas, which cannot be had for love or money, and I pick up canned goods that will keep me through my three days on Prince Edward Island, because they'll be easier to keep than frozen vegetables. I grab some jarred curry sauce, make sure it's vegetarian because it's often not, and flash back to the Hamburger Helper of my childhood camping. The food I'd had in the camper up to this point has mostly been cooked over the campfire, but the weather forecast on PEI is going to be too stormy for fires, so I need to reconsider Scamp Food, and I will actually start cooking. It won't be anything fancy, but the first step is using my little Crock-Pot. It will be several more years before I add a thrifted rice cooker to my Scamping appliances, so I'll have to rely on packaged instant rice.

When I get to the checkout with my cart, the look on the cashier's face is the mask of someone holding it together so tightly that when release comes it will shatter something inside of her.

It was his brother who was shot, she tells me, nodding to the tall man who has just exited the lane.

That's awful, I say. I don't need to know what she's talking about to find the situation terrible.

I walk back across the parking lot to where I parked the Jeep and the Scamp, stow the food in the camper, and pull back onto the road, not sure what I just walked through, and as I'm attempting to get onto Route 15 to Route 2, the roads are nearly empty in the direction I'm going and nobody in the oncoming lanes. It's incredibly eerie, but I have no frame of reference. In hindsight, it was wrong enough that I should have turned on the radio, but that didn't occur to me at the time. Maybe I just wondered if it was another sinkhole, another detour, like that day in Ontario. It felt different, though, and in hindsight I wonder why I didn't listen to my gut.

Police cruisers with flashing lights block the road in front of me, so I say a prayer of gratitude for the Jeep and Scamp's turning radius, turn around, and head back toward Moncton. This is the easiest and fastest way to get to Prince Edward Island, so I'll need to find an alternate path. Without conscious thought, what I'm doing is ignoring that history is literally happening right in front of me, intersecting with the road I'm on.

The gas station is empty when I pull in.

You look lost, says the attendant.

Not yet, I say, *but I'm getting there*. I say that they've shut down the road and I need another way to get to PEI.

Haven't you heard? he says. *Most of the city's shut down.*

Then he tells me about cops getting shot, and I say, *I'm not from here. I didn't know.*

He asks where I come from, in the voice of someone who expects that I would have had to be on Mars not to know what's going on. Later, I would imagine people camping on 9/11, coming back into a world that had changed utterly while they were unaware. I remember the unnatural silence of that day, the skies absent of planes over my apartment in Spokane, even road noise nearly eliminated as we processed what was happening. I say I've been in Fundy National Park for the last couple of days and he nods, as if this is acceptable ignorance. He pulls a newspaper off a shelf and hands it to me, where I read that a heavily armed twenty-four-year-old Justin Bourque had gone on a shooting spree that left three Mounties dead and two injured. The city shut down transit, businesses and schools closed, and Moncton turned into a ghost town while they searched for him, and it was this ghost town that I stumbled into on my way to somewhere else. Twenty-eight hours of citywide terror for Moncton, until Bourque gave himself up. But we don't know that now. Right now, we're fighting against fear.

The gas station attendant looks at me and says, *My advice, get out of town.* There's no snark in his voice. He's worried.

Trying, I say, more flippantly than I should have.

He gives me directions for an alternate route, and I pull back on the road. The ease with which I leave Moncton and its terror behind unsettles me a little, because I do have the privilege to simply drive away.

A COUPLE HOURS LATER, I OVERESTIMATE THE IMPACT OF driving across Confederation Bridge to Prince Edward Island, and it isn't nearly as exciting as I want it to be. Part of the problem with bridges of any magnitude while being a solo person driving is that you need to pay attention to the road instead of looking at the scenery. Rain starts when I leave Moncton, but it's cleared by the time I get to PEI, and the clarity of sky and water around the Confederation Bridge is like driving into eternity. And it is not interesting.

No sooner do I cross the bridge, noting how much it will cost me to leave the island—$45 + $7.50 per axle—than I am drowning in Anne of Green Gables kitsch, and I stare at the bottles of raspberry cordial, torn between actually wanting to buy some and feeling faintly nauseated at the pandering. This is high-quality pandering to the greatest of childhood nostalgia among us, and I'm not mad about it. I grew up on the 1985 *Anne of Green Gables*, Megan Follows, Jonathan Crombie, and Colleen Dewhurst, puffed sleeves and the exasperation of *twenty pounds of brown sugar*. Gilbert Blythe ruined all other men for me, I swear.

Prince Edward Island is a different kind of allure of elsewhere, and there's always a moment where you're standing in a place that you've only seen in movies or know from books, a world that is not real, and you think *wow, it really* does *exist*. I remember that reaction outside Radio City Music Hall, in front of the Declaration of Independence and the Golden Gate Bridge. Maybe that's enough of a reason to be here: because I'm curious, and the place is beautiful and wonderful, and I want to be here.

CABOT BEACH PROVINCIAL PARK MAY BE ONE OF THE FEW missteps in my nearly blind trust of Canadian provincial parks. It's mostly open, without many trees, and everything is old and worn. It's out of the way on the north side of the island, so I hope I haven't made a giant mistake, given the impending storm.

When I pull up to the gatehouse to register, I tell the woman inside that I want three nights, water and electric.

She looks at me, dumbfounded. *Have you* seen *the weather?*

I have. Nothing to be done about it.

She tells me to pick whatever site I want.

I nod and pull through.

I choose Site 9 and start to set up, making sure that the Scamp is level, putting chocks around the tires to keep it in place, cranking up the jack to take the camper off the Jeep hitch, and then I discover, to my horror, that it's on enough of an incline and the grass is wet and slippery enough that the Scamp, even with the chocks, slides gently down the incline and directly *into the back of the Jeep.*

I think I startle the local wildlife with my colorful language. Maeve gives me eight out of ten.

Thankfully, there's no damage to either, and once I recover from the horror of it, of trying to stop the slide of the Scamp with my own body—which, admittedly, is not my finest problem-solving hour—I'm grateful that the campground is empty enough of people that my humiliation will go unnoticed. I manage to reset the chocks, move the Jeep forward, and watch it slide down a second time.

Maeve gives me a nine out of ten.

There will not be a third time, so I hook it back up and head for the flat sites I should have picked the first time around.

Later that night, I realize that most people will never understand why I camp alone. They might eventually understand what compels me to travel, but they'll never understand what compels me to travel alone. They'll never understand what it's like to travel with everything in the world that I need hooked to my hitch or the absolute joy that comes with stretching out in my zero-gravity chair with a book in the middle of the afternoon, next to a piece of scenery I've never seen before—or in a place I've been so many times that it feels like it's part of my own mythology. They'll never understand why I'm so happy standing in the quiet of my camper in the brisk of morning, deciding what kind of tea I want to greet the day, then sitting on the picnic table and doing nothing except drinking my tea and breathing. It's pure, absolute freedom, but it's more complex than that; it's not a freedom *from*, it's a freedom *to*, a freedom *forward*. To do everything because I want to—and because I can.

Moments like this, I'm ridiculously glad to be camping alone, as evening descends onto the north shore of Prince Edward Island. I get ready for bed, all warm and comfortable as I snuggle down in the electric blanket with the cats. I hear the wind start to pick up, and the rain patters against the fiberglass in ever-increasing patterns, and then I realize, with a jolt, that in all the excitement of setting up the camper before it started to rain that I actually forgot to put down the stabilizer jacks. There's a gale coming. I've seen the weather. Not putting the jacks down is not an option. So, I mutter about useless cats not pulling their weight, camping alone, put my clothes and rain boots back on and do it. Because trying to sleep without the jacks down, with a storm coming, conditions are just going to get worse. And then I think that even if I wasn't camping alone, I wouldn't expect him to do the dirty work of getting cold and wet to put down the jacks, so I'd do it anyway. Because fair is fair. I'd never ask him to do something I'm not willing to do myself.

So, I do it, to the amusement of the crows who perch in the tree next to the Scamp and the cats, whose faces out the window speak of deep disappointment in humanity.

IN THE MORNING, THE WIND IS IN FULL FORCE, AND I'M glad to be inside fiberglass rather than the wet canvas of my childhood Starcraft pop-up. The weather seems to be more wind than rain so far, and I don't have any window leaks, which has happened many times before. If the weep holes in the windows are clogged, the windows will leak right onto my bed. This PEI weather is hardly a rain at all, so Irish in nature that I almost taste malty Assam in any of a dozen dark pubs in my memories. Many of my travel place-memories exist as literal flavors, so that weather patterns or angles of light or the movement of air taste of citrus or umami or spice. The rain here is more of a thick mist, tiny drops, with the force of wind turning it into something intense and sharp. The sky is one uniform shade of medium gray, so I can't even tell which direction the rain is moving, if it's moving, or if it's just sitting on top of us.

Yogurt and fresh raspberries are my breakfast at the front dinette, along with my tea. Mornings while camping taste of Rice Chex, the single solitary cereal our family of five could agree on. Raisins on our cereal. Mornings taste like Tang in a Tupperware jug we pretended was orange juice and thrilled at the novelty of it. We never got Tang at home. We rarely ate inside the pop-up, even on the coldest mornings, the picnic table spread with the flowered plastic tablecloth my parents still carry, the plastic Tupperware bowls and hand-me-down silverware. One spoon had a rose on it, and my sisters and I always fought over it. Whoever's day it was got to use it. A few years later, my parents will swap out the silverware in their camper; I snag the sentimental stuff, and it becomes my Scamp silverware. I won't have to fight anybody for the rose spoon.

Food in the Starcraft was about finding the balance between no refrigeration and frugality. We just had a red cooler that we always stored just inside the door of the camper when in transit and would refill with ice each day. We'd stop at rest stops for lunch, sandwiches and Pringles, because chips at home were really rare. Our lunch choices were either peanut butter and jelly or meat and cheese. Dad would cut the block of Colby on the top of the cooler with his Buck knife and inevitably make some sort of comment about not remembering if he'd cleaned it after gutting his last deer. Predictably, it grossed us out, as intended. After my sisters and I had run off some energy at the playground, we'd go back into the Blazer, or the Suburban that replaced the Blazer in later years, and settle in for another couple of hours toward our daily destination.

At some point, I realize that I'm not any less fussy in the camper—I just care about different things. Some people get precious about cooking on the stovetop—or the fire—when they camp, but I can't live without my microwave. A potato, scrubbed up and tucked into a little cloth envelope, is easy in the microwave. I can make better pastina in the microwave than I can on the stovetop. It's easier to make oatmeal and popcorn. I'd say I'm kind of lazy about food in the camper, but that's not exactly true. In the days before I left for Acadie, I pulled out the induction burner, set it on my parents' counter, and practiced all the meals I could make, so I knew if they worked or not. Maybe that takes away the anticipation, but I'd rather know I'm not going to go hungry.

———

As I LEAVE THE CAMPGROUND, I STOP AT THE entrance gate:

Any news on the Moncton shooter?

Yes, he gave himself up, she says.

I did not see that coming; I expected suicide by cop.

The woman nods. She didn't either.

The weather?

Yes, it's supposed to clear by tomorrow.

Nearest post office where I can mail my postcards?

She gives me directions.

My mother was the one who wrote postcards home to the kids when she and Dad went camping, but as he is learning what the world looks like without her, he's taken to sending his own postcards, which my sister is dutifully saving for the kids when they get older. Since so much of our communication is digital now, it's important that these little tangible bits of the family archive are still being created. Maybe it's that he let Mom do it because that was her instinct, and she was good at it; maybe it's that watching her do those tiny things that mean so much rubbed off on him after her death. I have a photo of four-year-old Cora holding up one of the postcards I sent from the Nova Scotia trip, pointing at the globe to where I am.

Three years later, I'll take her to Duluth over Memorial Day weekend. In preparation, I suggest she pack her rain boots.

Looks like there will be some puddles that require our attention, I say.

Cora makes a note on her packing list, which is secured to a clipboard too large for her tiny hands. She, like me, enjoys the trappings of organization.

Chance of storms all weekend.

She looks up. *Good*, she says. *I like storms better than rain.*

I channeled my mother and put together daily presents for her like Mom did for us when we went camping. She'd wrap up small things, like bubbles or a new game to play in the car, but it was meant to be shared by all three of us, and it was a moment of my mother thinking so far ahead toward how we could create memories that I'm still caught flat-footed at her invisible work.

I wanted to do the same for the niblings, so I thrifted a kid-sized blue backpack to hold a thrifted digital camera and Cora's very own Scamp journal, complete with new colored pencils, and as she was not a proficient writer, I suggested she draw a picture of what we did that day. I'll do the same for Henry and Sam when they're old enough. The Scamp Camera has turned out to be a hit—they can take as many pictures as they want and it doesn't cost any film or developing, and for their birthdays, I turn their own pictures into a small photo book for our memories. It's a visual way we're turning those memories into a story we can tell later, just like the postcards I'm faithfully sending back on this trip.

I don't expect to encounter anything Babine on PEI, particularly because none of my family records place us on PEI at any point, but I stop at several churches to walk their churchyards in my polka-dot rain boots, and it doesn't bother me that I can't read any of the gravestones in French. These are not my people, but they still tell the story of this place in a way that *Anne of Green Gables* didn't. On the way back to the Scamp, it was the small cemetery in Malpeque Bay that pulls the Jeep to the side of the road. The cemetery is very Scottish, I discover, which contrasts with the French and Irish of the other island cemeteries.

I don't romanticize cemeteries, because they're such an important part of how I've constructed the family archive; cemeteries in Ireland are one of my favorite ways to spend an afternoon. Cemeteries are the data that tells me what the original language of the colonizing settlers was, and just by watching the gravestones I can see when that language shifted into English. I've walked the cemetery at Chisago Lake Lutheran Church in Center City, Minnesota, the stronghold of my Swedish ancestors, where my three-greats grandparents, Lars[3] and Ingre Thorsander[3] are buried, sharing a stone with their son Peter, who dropped dead of a heart attack at his kitchen table at the age of thirty-three. His wife remarried and is buried elsewhere. I've traced my fingers over the *hvila i frid* on the grave of my three-greats grandfather Oke Dahlberg[3], who died in 1926 at the age of 100, with his wife Bothilda. I know that *född i Sverige* means born in Sweden, even though my own Swedish is rusty. Over the decades, the language evolves into English in ways I can also trace in my own family history. It's not even that I hunt cemeteries for stories I know are there, or the stories untold, or how they record stories. The graves of my great-uncle Walt and great-grandmother Catherine say nothing about how they came to be there, and I remember the exchange between my father and grandfather at their funeral:

If I didn't tell them I loved them in life, it makes no sense to do it now.

And yet, after my grandmother Marion died, my grandfather visited her grave every week and that seemed right too.

I very, very rarely feel anything in cemeteries—one notable exception being the mass grave of the Irish on Grosse Île in Quebec. But here, at the small cemetery in Malpeque, the grief nearly chokes me. I don't usually have this kind of reaction, but it is deep and it is visceral and it is very real.

James Woodside, lost at sea, 1919.

John McKay, age fifty-four, drowned, April 6, 1876.

Twin brothers Jacob and Thomas Clark, drowned, July 22, 1852.

Francis H. Shields, buried in France, April 20, 1918. His wife, Annie, died in 1981.

Buried elsewhere.

Lost at sea.

Flight Sergeant Gerald F. McNutt, missing in action, May 15, 1942.

A monument to the twelve unknown American seamen buried here.

Even as I'm standing there, a quote from my favorite Irish essayist, Tim Robinson, occurs to me:

I like fossicking and yoricking about in graveyards, scanning the headstones, stopping for a closer look at one or another, as one takes down a book from a bookshop shelf to see if its opening words live up to its title. One of my desiderata for a well-run world would be that every tombstone carry a brief biography (and, at the foot, "For notes and sources, see over").

I consider fossicking and yoricking as I wander these stones in the mist, thinking about the waves of the land at the mass grave on Grosse Île, about how the collective stories in these stones function differently than the individual.

━━

LATER, I DRIVE ROUTE 2 TOWARD CHARLOTTETOWN TO follow the top half of the Anne of Green Gables / Central Scenic Tour. I'm sure it's lovely, but I can't see the coast for the rain, and it feels a lot like my Alma wanderings: the experience feels like an object to be collected. I avoid the Anne of Green Gables tourist traps, and instead I park across the street from the cemetery where L. M. Montgomery is buried. I don't go hunting for her grave immediately, though. I go wandering first. When I do find it, it's freshly planted with bright begonias, but I never know what to do at the graves of historical figures. Am I paying respects? I don't even know what that means. It mostly feels like a moment to check off an invisible checklist.

This cemetery has a much different feel than the others I visited—here I see too many children, too many women of obvious childbearing age. It's easy to think of infant and maternal mortality as products of a bygone era, when both are currently on the rise after the fall of Roe. Women still face these dangers, and it's much more dangerous for women of color, but it's not as it was for our grandmothers and great-grandmothers, as it was for Mary[2], Julienne[3], Victoire[4], Elisabeth[5], Cécile[6], Anne Marie[7], Anne[8], and Marie[9] Babin. Most mothers would have lost at least one child—not even counting miscarriages, which are rarely recorded in the data. I see it every time I spend time in the genealogical records, dates that line up too closely. It makes me wonder about what's not written down, like my great-grandfather's death certificate reading *accident*, so he could be buried in consecrated ground. Catherine's death certificate reads *homicide*. So does Walt's. Homicide is the leading cause of death for pregnant women in the United States, and I wonder how far back that goes into what's not recorded. I wonder which stones would read cancer, or childbirth, or car accident if we let them, and I wonder what difference it would make if they did. Maybe none.

It's hard not to read these documents and gravestones without a twenty-first-century mindset. In one record, above the entry in the family Bible for the birth of my grandfather and his twin, there's an entry for a boy—stillborn, November 14, 1923. Grandpa and Walt would arrive eleven months later, which means she'd only miscarried two months before she became pregnant again. I wonder if the baby was buried, if he was buried outside consecrated ground because he was unbaptized, I wonder if my great-grandfather was responsible for the burial of his stillborn son as men often were in those days, and I wonder about the kindness of the medical examiner twenty years in the future that would allow that baby's father eternal rest of the sanctioned kind. Bill Sr. and Catherine were Catholic, and the loss of their child was decades before the Catholic Church recognized the abject human cruelty of unbaptized children in limbo, of not allowing their burial in consecrated ground.

The Catholic Church had strong opinions on right ways and wrong ways to do children. My grandparents married on April 4, 1948, in a flash of sweet peas, Marion's brilliant smile, and my grandfather looking at her as they walked back down the aisle like he couldn't believe how he got so lucky. The way he looked at her—it's everything you'd want in that moment. Walt and Ada married just three weeks later, and my dad says Marion always felt like they stole her bridal spotlight. Ada was also four months pregnant, with David born six months before my father, which my father also imagines stole Marion's attention as the rightful bearer of the first grandchild. That tracks. My grandmother was unforgiving about that kind of thing. There was a right way to do things and a wrong way to do things.

But here's the moment of embodied history I return to: My grandmother miscarried between Brian and Teresa, something I had heard once, but nothing anyone would talk about to help me fill in more details, so I'm not even sure when it happened. Dad doesn't remember much about the time, except that she was very sick, and from my memory, I think she was seven or eight months along, far enough that my dad knew she was pregnant. It's a literally embodied hurt she kept private, a child she carried alone, and there's something deeply human and vulnerable about that kind of loss, especially for a woman who never let anyone but my grandfather close. I wish I knew if my grandfather grieved the loss too. Women carry fetal cells decades after birth, so her lost daughter was never in the past for my grandmother, and I think about all the miscarriages of women in my family, my mother, grandmothers, my great-grandmother Catherine, the embodied history they carried, because those kind of stories were private, sometimes not even discussed between close family and friends, and I think about the lines between silencing and privacy, and the loneliness of that kind of grief.

How do we talk about the wonder that the cells that would become my cousins were already inside my aunt Teresa when Marion was pregnant with her?

At my grandmother's funeral, a year after I return from Nova Scotia, she will leave a letter to be read in which she refers to the baby as Marion. Afterward, in the intense tree-less heat of a California September, I say to my father and grandfather that I didn't know the baby's name was Marion. *I didn't either,* my grandfather says, a bit bewildered.

━━━

AT THE EGLISE NOTRE DAME DU MONT CARMEL ON Prince Edward Island, which is Acadian in origin, the stark-ness of white gravestones against the blue-gray of the storm just offshore is intense. I can't read any of the inscriptions, but what's particularly arresting about this churchyard is the blank space down the center of the rows of gravestones, and I'm reminded of Grosse Île again, that a landscape can tell a story without words. A large marker reads *Identified Children Buried in This Cemetery with Unknown Graves,* and among the list of names of those children they know, the list of *enfant anonyme* is so long. Was this once unconsecrated ground, newly consecrated? Or did it remain in limbo? But the lack of markers, the *enfant anonyme,* speaks to me of the unknowing, the untelling, and the physical evidence—or lack thereof—of planned forgetting.

There's so much silence around women and child-bearing, the choice of children, the choice of when to bear those children. It's hard not to look at the records of my foremothers and all the children they bore and rest my own worldview on them, projecting a lack of power onto their lives, their marriages at sixteen, motherhood at the whim of husbands who were decades older, a rural life that demanded as many children as possible to serve as family labor. Just because it's a life I would have chafed against, one that likely would have broken me, it's problematic to assume that the women in my ancestral line would have felt the same. What if they had exactly the life they wanted? Sometimes I wonder about the construction of families, what's only left behind in the records, what records a hundred years from now might say about me. I expect they will say little. Pope Francis recently said that a life with only pets and no children is an unfulfilled life, empty, a refrain he will return to many times. I'm not Catholic, but it's difficult not to stand in this physical place and this place in time, where the lives of women are measured by their relationships to other people, to husbands, to children, instead of on their own individual merits as human beings, and it's difficult to shake that feeling right now. I'm not in a bad mood as I get back in the Jeep, but I'm close. I'm tired of being told my life has no meaning or value because I'm not married and don't have children. It comes from so many directions, and it's exhausting.

When I return to the Scamp, the cats are asleep on the bed. This life is not unfulfilled, not even close to empty. This is the best kind of life.

The campground is still pretty quiet. The Aliner is still here, but I haven't seen any people. With the weather I wouldn't be outside either. The Class C next to me left this morning, and there's another Class C two rows over. I turn on the heater, make myself a pot of tea, and settle in at the front dinette to download my pictures to my computer. It can't all be good weather, but at least there's no wet canvas.

The weather starts to clear a little bit as we approach the dinner hour, so I pull out my little Crock-Pot and fill it with a jar of curry sauce, a potato, an onion, half a can of chickpeas, and half a can of peas and carrots. I make sure I'm not going to burn down the Scamp and then load up my camera to go down to the beach to see what there is to see. The wind is strong, but the visibility is much improved. The tide is out, and it's still storm-cold, but I stay out there for a while, breathing gray skies and red sand.

Later, tucked up at the front dinette with my dinner, with Maeve on the opposite seat, both of us staring at the gray out the front window, I think about travel stories and how we tell them, how we remember the flavor of them on our tongues, and just how many of our best family stories are food and travel, and I wonder what it means that I could trace my dad's Air Force travel through food. Sangria and paella in Spain. Steak in Uruguay. I wonder if his memories have flavors for him, in the way that mine do. Mushrooms put me on the Aran Islands, yellow curry on PEI, Maritime Mist tea at Mackinac Island.

I think about how his stories, though not in combat zones, have the same feel as the World War II stories of my grandfathers—amusing and of little substance. Maybe food stories stick because they are visceral, not just sensory, a moment literally taken into our bodies, broken down, and filtered into our cells. Is this how genetic memory works? That perhaps I carry that T-bone steak in my cells, passed down from my father? Do I carry the bread full of weevils from my maternal grandfather's Coast Guard convoy in the South Pacific? Do I carry the legacy of Yarmouth fisheries, Acadian grain? What flavors will remind me of this place and the experiences I have consumed here?

IN THE MORNING, THE SUN IS BRIGHT ENOUGH THAT I AM very tempted to stay another day on Prince Edward Island, but I cannot. Halifax is calling in Acadian voices, even though I do not know at the time that there are Babines among them. The drive to the Confederation Bridge is magnificent in the sunshine, and I feel a certain regret in leaving.

CHAPTER ELEVEN

I F YOU GOOGLE *WRECKWOOD*, WHAT COMES UP IS LARGELY
Titanic. So many of the ships lost to wreck were not as
famous as *Titanic*, and I imagine that the splinters and
fragments that found their way to the stores of Nova Scotia
never could be identified to a particular ship. Years later,
I'll find a Reddit thread in which the poster found a desk
made from the wreckwood of SS *Iowa*, which sank in an
incredible storm as it was outbound from the Columbia
River in 1936. It was driven onto Peacock Spit by gale-force
winds, and despite the efforts of the lighthouse keeper, the
storm was too fierce to mount a rescue. Thirty-four crew
perished, and it is still considered one of the worst maritime disasters of the twentieth century on the Columbia
River Bar. From the wreckwood of the *Iowa*, the lighthouse keeper made a desk in the lost crewmates' memory.
So much lumber was salvaged from the ship that it sparked
a small housing boom in the area, as the story goes. The
Redditor commented that the clerk at St. Vincent de Paul
was glad to see it gone, as she believed it was haunted and
recounted several ghost encounters when near the desk.

Adrienne Rich comes to mind:

the thing I came for:
the wreck and not the story of the wreck
the thing itself and not the myth
the drowned face always staring
toward the sun
the evidence of damage
worn by salt and sway into this threadbare beauty
the ribs of the disaster
curving their assertion
among the tentative haunters.

My primary purpose in Halifax is *Titanic*, not specifically family, but like much of what I will find in Acadie, the
story I'm looking for is resisting itself. I go to find *Titanic*,
yet I'll leave with something else entirely.

I was deeply obsessed with *Titanic* in high school, to
the point where I watched the movie once and it was so
deeply traumatic to put faces to stories and details I knew
so well that I never watched it again. I researched her sister ships, the *Britannic* and the *Olympic*, and I wondered
about the maritime stories that sailors tell, wondered about
curses. I collected data like stones, could spout off trivia
like a champ. I went to every museum exhibit I could. In
2013, I'd find myself at the Belfast shipyards where *Titanic*
and her sisters were built, standing in the shadow of those
giant cranes named Samson and Goliath, even as souvenirs
boasted *Titanic: she was fine when she left here!* or *Titanic:
built by the Irish, sunk by the British.* I'd spent time inside
the Titanic Belfast Experience, one of the most interesting
interactive historical experiences I've ever encountered;
"nine interactive galleries where you discover the sights,
sounds, smells and stories of the ship, as well as the people

and city that made her," boasts its website. I'd been to Cobh, Ireland, her last port.

The fragments of experience would eventually lead to something whole, or so I hoped. It felt necessary, somehow, to stand in those places, regardless of what I would take away with me when I left.

The *Titanic* dead were brought to Halifax, while the survivors went to New York, and something in me wants the tangibility of that time, to walk their graves, and that's my reason for spending a few days in Halifax. What I find, though, is even more tangible, more quotidian, and not what I expected. Behind glass at the Maritime Museum of the Atlantic in Halifax, there's a rolling pin made from *Titanic* wreckwood by J. A. O'Brien, cable engineer aboard the *Mackay-Bennett*, one of the ships sent to rescue survivors and collect the dead. The artifact note says that the rolling pin was donated by O'Brien's daughter, and I imagine this moment of a family rolling out pie crusts with the wood of the *Titanic*. It seems so morbid, so needlessly melancholic. I can't imagine the happiness of Christmas, snow and evergreen and mulled cider, and rolling out sugar cookies, knowing what memories that rolling pin held. Or the picture frame made from wreckwood next to it on the shelf—what inescapable story do the fragments tell that can't be written over?

It's easy to think of histories, and cemeteries, and museums—like Malpeque, or Grosse Île, or even what I will find a few days from now in Kennebunk, Maine—as dead, as fixed and finite, as no longer actively making meaning, but the truth is that such a belief denies that these places and objects are existing in the current moment, there on the shelf, under their full spectrum lighting, and that

each person who comes into contact with them is actively
making new meaning in the encounter.

—

THE COMPLICATION OF HALIFAX IS THAT IT COMES OUT OF
order, as I've now crossed into territory that has Babin footprints on it. I should have gone to Grand-Pré first, then
Halifax, then Yarmouth, but I don't know at the time that
we had ever been in Halifax.

the thing itself and not the myth

At the time, I do not know the Babins had been imprisoned in Halifax. All I have are fragments in this bit
of Babin history, back to 1755 and the deportations of the
Acadians, the imprisonment of brothers Pierre Babin[6] and
Joseph Babin with Pierre Surette[6], and the deportation
of Pierre Babin[6] and Joseph Babin's parents and siblings.
This period, from 1755 to about 1770, is difficult to piece
together. The records don't exist, or they're in a language I
can't read, or I don't know where to find them. What I don't
have are any records from Halifax, though Father Clarence
d'Entremont observes that the Surettes and Babins were
kept prisoner until the end of the Seven Years' War in 1763.
I know that my five-greats grandfather, Joseph Olivier dit
Carino Babin[5] was born there in 1768 and would have been
about a year old when the family, along with Pierre Surette[6],
made the move to Yarmouth. I expect that Pierre Babin's[6]
brother Joseph married Pierre Surette's[6] daughter Madeline
while in Halifax, maybe at the Citadel itself, because the
records indicate that Pierre Surette[6] went to Yarmouth with

his sons-in-law. There's no mention of Cécile[6] and Pierre Babin[6] making the move, but I don't have death information for them either. I've never found records for more of their children other than Marie and Joseph[5] so if they survived Halifax, they didn't add to their family when they settled in Yarmouth. My own assumption is that Pierre[6] and Cécile[6] died in Halifax.

Maybe all I can construct, in the end, is a different kind of family myth from the wreckwood in front of me.

━━

STILL IN SEARCH OF *TITANIC*, I PARK THE JEEP AT THE Fairview Lawn Cemetery near where the *Titanic* dead are buried and step out into shaded sunshine to take stock. I know that 121 *Titanic* victims are buried here in three curves of gray granite stones designed by E. W. Christie and that the way is well marked. What I'm not quite sure of is why it's so important to see them—maybe an odd kind of closure.

the ribs of the disaster / curving their assertion

I don't know what I want in this moment at Fairview Lawn Cemetery, because I don't get it. When I start making my way toward the *Titanic* graves, I get distracted.

In Loving Memory of Florence May, beloved wife of W. B. Williams, Killed by Explosion, December 6, 1917, aged 22 years.

In memory of my wife and children, Emily Robinson, Raymond, Florence, Killed in Halifax Explosion, December 6, 1917.

Then another.

Frank Davis, died in 1953, his wife Lena and their son Charles both *Killed in Hfx Explosion.*

I turn a little, and there is another. *George R., born Banffshire, Scotland, April 15, 1891, his sister Jessie D., aged*

15 years, children of Wm. and Jane Aitkin, killed by explosion, December 6, 1917.

Another.

What am I looking at?

What had happened?

In Memory of Wm. M. Vaughn, aged 38 years, his wife Catherine L, aged 36. Died December 6, 1917.

Every time I turn a fraction, there is another.

I might have come to this place for the *Titanic*, but I find the *Mont-Blanc* instead.

I don't know how to measure the largest human-caused preatomic explosion in my mind, because it's larger than my scope: the bustle of a busy war port, the *Mont-Blanc* laden with explosives bound from New York to France, the Norwegian *Imo* en route to pick up relief supplies in New York. Later I'll wish I had taken time to drive the area and see the scars in the land, but at the time I don't realize that where I've started my morning, at the Maritime Museum of the Atlantic, is so close to the Narrows, where it happened. On the morning of December 6, 1917, the *Imo* seems not to have followed the protocols of the Narrows and collided with the *Mont-Blanc*, which was carrying TNT, picric acid, benzol, and guncotton. From what I understand, the *Mont-Blanc* itself was not seriously damaged, but the barrels of benzol on deck broke open and caught fire—twenty minutes later, a half-mile radius around the Narrows was wiped from the map. The shock wave was felt as far away as Prince Edward Island. The resulting tsunami carried the *Imo* onto land in Dartmouth. Sixteen hundred people were killed in the initial explosion, more succumbed to their wounds later, and a further nine thousand were injured. The Tufts Cove area of Dartmouth, home to a community of Mi'kmaq since the

1700s, was obliterated. They say the death toll could have been much larger if not for the quick thinking of a railway dispatcher named Patrick Vincent Coleman, who understood what was happening aboard the burning *Mont-Blanc* and sent a telegraph to an incoming passenger train, the record of which is preserved at the Maritime Museum of the Atlantic:

> *Hold up the train. Ammunition ship afire in harbor making for Pier 6 and will explode. Guess this will be my last message. Good-bye boys.*

The story goes that the message made its way to the other incoming trains, including one carrying three hundred passengers. Coleman was killed by the explosion. What lingers in all my readings about the explosion is how many survivors were blinded by the blast, hundreds of them, largely from glass shards and other shrapnel. A 2007 article in the *British Journal of Ophthalmology* titled "The Halifax disaster (1917): eye injuries and their care" details the work of local eye doctors to treat the horrific injuries caused by flying glass.

It's easy, again, to separate history into its fragments and its puzzle pieces and forget that, in 1917, my great-grandfather Bill Sr., born in Yarmouth, was already drafted into the American army, training in Texas, and likely preparing to ship to France. The rest of the family was settled in Kennebunk, Maine. The news of the explosion in Halifax would have certainly reached him wherever he was, and I don't imagine the news landed lightly. Halifax would likely have been a place he knew. The family, in Maine, would have felt the shock wave.

It's one thing to memorize how many died, how many thousands of homes were destroyed or damaged, how many people were left homeless, left without jobs, because the industrial area of Halifax was gone, most of its workers dead—but I come back to the humanity of the story: it was December in the Maritimes. Cold. Winter. Three weeks away from Christmas. Civilians. In the midst of the Great War. I wonder again about *the shrapnel of family tragedy* and wonder about the shrapnel of war, of the *Mont-Blanc*, of rebuilding the area in the decades after the explosion. We can rebuild, but remembering is built into the fabric of the place. I wonder, too, about Halifax being the site of such fragmenting.

———

TITANIC AND THE *MONT-BLANC* DON'T HAVE ANYTHING OB-vious to do with the Acadians or the Babins, but I keep coming back to Adrienne Rich, like a mantra I'm repeating over and over in my head like it will keep me grounded:

> *the thing I came for:*
> *the wreck and not the story of the wreck*
> *the thing itself and not the myth*

Father Clarence d'Entremont, the Acadian historian and genealogist, writes in "The Escape of the Acadians from Fort Lawrence at the Time of the Expulsion" that the ac-count of escape from Fort Lawrence comes from the grand-son of a prisoner, who heard it from his grandfather in the passing down of stories as warning, as a call to be prepared, that if the story is lost, the community loses what it needs to keep itself safe. I find myself grateful that these stories have not been lost, because they no longer exist down the family line of Babines, and they are stories I wish I'd been told. But it's hard to blame them for not telling them.

Though the rumblings of *le Grand Dérangement* started decades earlier, Father Clarence d'Entremont tells two stories, which begin when, on

July 23, 1755, Charles Lawrence, governor of Nova Scotia, sent secretly a message to all the military posts in the Province that it had been decided to do away with the Acadians by embarking them in vessels and sending them abroad, mainly on the coast of what is now the United States.

A couple of weeks later, all the men living in the vicinity of Amherst were summoned to gather at Fort Beausejour, to discuss matters relating to the Oath of Allegiance to the Sovereign of England. On the 11 of August, 250 Acadians arrived at the fort, all men, and were immediately incarcerated. As they were too numerous to be held in one fort, the majority were sent the same day to Fort Lawrence. The following weeks, other Acadians were apprehended, and it kept on up to the month of October. This is, in fact, what we read in Dr. John Thomas' diary, which he kept at the time. On August 11, he writes: "Colonel Muncton got 250 of the inhabitants into Fort Cumberland and confined them Major Bourn with 150 men guarding the greater part of them to Fort Lawrence where they are confined."

Whether or not the meeting was a ruse, I don't know. Seems likely. Maybe the English knew the Acadians would balk at the unqualified oath, and that would be enough excuse to deport them. Maybe it was just to get all the people in one place, as Colonel John Winslow had done in September 1755, when he arrived in Grand-Pré with a message from the king, summoned the men to the church and announced the large scale deportation of the Acadians.

The arrests continued through October. Father d'Entremont continues:

> *In 1755, [Pierre Surette[6]] was living in Beausejour, located on the border between Nova Scotia and New Brunswick, when the Acadians of that region were summoned to appear at Fort Beausejour on August 11 of that year. As I was telling you last week, 250 answered the call. But a number, apprehending that it was some kind of a scheme, took to the woods. Pierre II Surette[6] and a number of others, who intended to hide in the woods, tarried too long behind and were captured and taken to Fort Beausejour.*

In December, my six-greats grandfather Pierre Surette[6] was imprisoned at Fort Beauséjour. He was forty-six years old, married for twenty-three years to Catherine Breau[6], and the father of nine children. With him were my six-greats grandfather Pierre Babin[6] and his brother Joseph. Pierre Babin[6] was twenty-five, Joseph sixteen. The story goes that the prisoners were fed horse meat, and it was Pierre Surette's[6] idea to save some of the bones and use them to dig a tunnel to escape. Father d'Entremont writes of Father François Le Guerne, missionary to the imprisoned Acadians, who wrote to the Governor of Louisbourg:

> *I hold this (information) from Pierre Surette[6] . . . This man, formerly a captain in the militia of Petcoudiac, is sensible and of good judgment, and well versed in public affairs,*

and was often employed by our Messieurs Officers in delicate matters. The English had kept him this winter at the fort as a man of reason who knew the country and might be useful to them. His agreeable manner of speech gave him a free access to the Commander of the fort (Mr. Scot), who thought him secure, so much so, that he spoke his mind openly to him. He knows the English language and is ever ready to converse with anyone, and they were in the habit of holding nothing in reserve when talking with him.

I picture Pierre Surette[6] as a big man, a strong man in his midforties, in his prime, clever enough to play both sides. Or that's the story I'm telling for myself, because I like the idea of Pierre being a bit of a spy. Of course, I have no way of knowing how it all went down. It's December in the Maritimes, full of cold and snow and storms blowing in off the Atlantic. I don't imagine that the prisoners would have been well taken care of. I imagine Pierre Babin[6], young and strong and his bones full of fire and fear at his parents' and siblings' deportation while he and his brother were imprisoned, not yet knowing he'd never see them again. I always imagine them strong, my ancestors: no childhood illnesses or injuries, no cancer, no scarlet fever, or tetanus, or migraines, no back problems, no depression or schizophrenia or PTSD or suicide or murder. No phobias or allergies. They're always rather perfect in my imagination, strong and attractive and skilled and brave, a blank slate on which to hang my ideas of who I hope they were. It's statistically probable that some—if not many—of my ancestors were monsters, that a good number of them were trapped in deeply unhappy marriages. I keep trying to paint them as noble with no real evidence for it. They wanted to survive, and the brain and body do what they must. I wonder what it did to them, hiding in the Maritime woods after they escaped, watching their loved ones starve, freeze. They watched their fractured community splinter even further, human wreckwood, *le Grand Dérangement* stretching into the next generation, then the next, beyond what they could see, toward California, toward the future.

In late February, the tunnel was complete, and all eighty men escaped. There was a moment when Pierre Melanson, who was apparently rather large, got stuck in the tunnel, but they were able to extract him in time. The English raised the alarm, but the Acadians knew the woods better than the English did, and they were able to escape. D'Entremont writes that "after two years of misery and starvation, eating roots, the meat of decayed animals, and even the excrement of animals as we are told by Father Le Guerne, these Acadians went around Miramichi, where their condition proved to be worse. Finally, they were obliged to surrender, that which took place around Petcoudiac and Memramcook, November 18, 1759."

Then they were sent to prison in Halifax. Maybe they were sent to the Citadel, but if so, those are records I will have to leave without knowing, and the history that Father d'Entremont has collected slides into myth, into a story I can only reconstruct from fragments and imagination.

HOURS LATER, WHILE I'M THINKING OF THESE FRAGMENTS and myths inside the natural history museum, it's the photographic exhibit of the horses of Sable Island that pulls me closer, not the specimens of turtles and birds and fish in glass cases. Sable Island is a place I know nothing about, but the wild horses here pull the wild horses from *Misty of Chincoteague* from my memory. I later wonder just how many childhood books featured in my Acadian wanderings in one way or another. Sable Island, I will learn, is part of the Graveyard of the Atlantic, an area responsible for at least 350 shipwrecks. This is dangerous territory. In these moments, the history of wreckwood in this place makes more sense.

> *the thing I came for:*
> *the wreck and not the story of the wreck*
> *the thing itself and not the myth*

Nobody lives on Sable Island, a sliver of an island located 160 kilometers off the coast of Nova Scotia, which is populated, at last count, by five hundred wild horses. Their origin story is murky, whether they swam ashore after being shipwrecked or were simply left there, but it seems the prevailing theory is that they were seized from the Acadians as they were being deported to Boston. DNA testing of the horses confirms their Acadian ancestry. It is these photographs of these shaggy horses, stolen and abandoned and thriving, that gives me pause. I'm looking at living, breathing wreckwood, and something inside me wants to say something ridiculous, like *hello*.

———

THE NEXT MORNING, THE SCAMP AND CATS ARE SNUG AT our campground in Halifax as I put the Jeep to the road and go be a tourist in search of pretty things, to counteract the weight of the day before. Peggy's Cove is popular with tourists, picturesque, and I have no problem being drawn in by the promise of a view promised to others. The drive along the coast is spectacular and puts me in mind of Lake Superior, the bare Canadian Shield, the intensity of water. The sun is bright, and though I get a bit lost on the cove roads, I don't mind. What else do I have to do?

Peggy's Cove is all ice age granite, scored and worn, boulders tossed like toys, bedrock round like the back of a whale. The visitor's center is quite helpful, and I walk past the most extraordinary carving in the boulders, William E. deGarthe's depiction of thirty-two fishermen with their wives and children under the protection of St. Elmo, along with Peggy of Peggy's Cove herself.

I walk the short distance through the village to the lighthouse, wondering at the light itself, both sharp and gold, unusual for a midsummer midday. It's easy to romanticize the salt-worn wood, the peeling paint, the entire New England fishing village vibe that comes from books and movies. It's a raw place, one I can imagine gets pummeled by many a good nor'easter and tastes of oysters and warm potatoes. Houses appear laid gently into the sharp hills, the granite of the Canadian Shield peeking bare among green grass. I don't know why the contrast of granite hits me so hard in my bones, but it does, whether it's Grosse Île or here. I walk through a study of deep color on the way to the lighthouse: green grass, blue sky, yellow and red houses. It's low tide; high tide must be its own treat, the pylons covered, the floating docks floating. The lighthouse is impressive, as they always are, rising strong from the granite. I remember what I've read about rogue waves at Peggy's Cove as I see the warning signs for people not to get too close to the edge, lest the unsuspecting and unwise be swept out to sea. *Stay off the black rocks,* the signs warn. *Savor the sea from a distance.* There was a short-lived Twitter account that aimed to raise awareness of tourists doing stupid things too close to the water by calling out the Morons of the Cove, but it makes me wonder about what calls humans so close to the edge, despite all warnings.

It's starting to cloud up a little when I leave Peggy's Cove and head toward Lunenberg, but I don't really think much of it. When I finally get there, the temperature has dropped noticeably. I consume Lunenberg quickly, collecting city blocks and images and impressions and putting them in my mental pockets for later, rationalizing that I'll give myself something to come back to, the collecting of an experience for the sake of it, much like a few days ago in Alma. It's lovely and perfect here, like a movie set, the same way that Peggy's Cove felt.

Lunenberg is a UNESCO World Heritage Site, a British colonial settlement that was drawn up and planned in England before it ever became a reality in Acadie, and it is architecturally charming, picturesque—all the adjectives that I would give to an experience of all image and no substance. It is a story imposed on a space, written elsewhere and constructed on a landscape that was already thick with stories. Something about maritime architecture is deeply attractive to me in a way I've never been able to explain and part of me doesn't want to. Lunenberg was founded in 1753, two years before *le Grand Dérangement*, and this sours my walking of the streets. Intellectually, I know my bad mood is the result of low blood sugar, but that doesn't matter in the moment. I buy a pottery pitcher made of local red Nova Scotia clay and a small mug that will make my newly purchased tea taste even better. I pass a plaque that reads:

This was a French cemetery when the foreign Protestants arrived in 1753. Today only 19th century monuments remain. 18th century gravestones are to be found in Hillcrest Cemetery on Gallows Hill.

There are no Babins, to my knowledge, in Lunenberg, so the cemetery itself is not on my list, though it will later be a moment of recognition, realizing that the Acadian graves would have lost their wooden markers long ago.

the thing I came for:
the wreck and not the story of the wreck
the thing itself and not the myth

The streets of Lunenberg are straight and planned and perfect, and it makes my brain itch. Maybe it's the rigid nature of the story that Lunenberg has been constructed to tell. Or been allowed to tell. There's power in story—and power in controlling what kinds of stories are available.

The schooner *Bluenose II* is moored in the bay, and my memories flick to the hookers of Galway, Ireland, that I know so well: hookers, the *oo* like *boo*, the boat native to that stretch of the Irish shoreline. I remember seeing a hooker called *Truelight* in Roundstone a few years back and wondering for a fleeting moment whether it was the same *Truelight* that had been the only ship to survive the 1927 Cleggan Bay Disaster—a freak gale that blew up the coast of Galway and killed forty-five fishermen, decimating the small community. In talking with the man working the boat, I learned that the *Truelight* was long gone, but this one was named for it.

So you know the history, he said.

I know a little bit of the history, I said.

I wonder about maritime tragedies, what it's like to send your family members out onto the water each day, not knowing if they'll return. In Galway, the swans that populate the Claddagh, the sixth-century fishing village that formed the foundation for the city, are considered to be the souls of the fishermen returned.

There's something deeply affecting about the black of a hull against the water. I don't know anything about boats, couldn't tell you if the boat I was looking at was a schooner or a brig or painted in the harmonies of "Sloop John B." My experience of boats is confined to my Minnesota grandparents' dock at Third Crow Wing Lake, the weather systems they call Alberta clippers, the ore boats on Lake Superior. I wonder where the original *Bluenose* is, and I think about replicas, about recreations in honor of a past moment worth remembering, about what we create out of the wreckwood we collect. Are the archives of a family just the wreckwood of who we were at one point in time? The original *Bluenose*, I come to know, was a racing schooner built in Nova Scotia who, over the course of her life, was undefeated. She was eventually sold and unfortunately wrecked in Haiti, but the *Bluenose II* came to succeed her. I also learn that bluenose is a nickname for Nova Scotians, going back into the eighteenth century.

The truth is that I can't look at the *Bluenose II* without seeing the *Dolphin*, the sloop that took Joseph Babin[7] and Anne Marie Landry[7], three of their children, and Joseph's brothers and their families from Acadie in late October 1755 and dumped them in Maryland at the end of November. The story goes that the *Dolphin*, along with several other transport ships, ran into weather and had to seek shelter in Boston before continuing to Maryland, which delayed her and depleted the already-minimal supplies for her passengers, who were overloaded in the ship. Some sources estimate that death tolls on many of the ships was as high as 50 percent.

The rain starts in earnest as I leave Lunenberg, and I drive back to the Scamp in the rain. I don't mind, as my mood matches the weather, a little dark, a little melancholy, a little angry, but then I remember that I'd left the windows open because it had gotten stuffy in there for the cats yesterday, so naturally my bedding is soaking wet when I get back to the Scamp. So, with my parents' memories of doing the same in Thunder Bay, I spend the evening in my campground's laundry, drying out my bedding, wondering again about history repeating itself.

CHAPTER TWELVE

THE DRIVE FROM HALIFAX TO YARMOUTH DOWN THE
Atlantic side of the peninsula is music in my blood,
lupins bright in the ditches, sun catching in the mist.
When Highway 103 ends in Yarmouth, I stop at a gas
station, mostly because Galway has expressed his gastric
displeasure at being cooped up in his kennel. It's possible
Maeve stopped yelling at me at some point, but I've gotten
good at tuning her out after the first half hour.

When I go inside to pay for my gas, I ask for directions to my campground. I'm told that the bridge is out and
there's a detour, and I feel the kind of exhaustion I recognize from Thunder Bay, just the feeling that my brain has
been shaken against my skull for too long—and so three of
them try to figure out directions for me to get there. Then a
couple of customers come in, join the conversation, each of
them with a different set of directions. Finally, the woman
who seems to be in charge lets the young man off work a
little early because he lives out the way I'm headed, and he
basically leads me straight to Ellenwood Lake Provincial
Park where I do not end up staying after all, because none of
the sites have electricity, and I require electricity. So I pull

out the Good Sam directory, and there's only one listing for Yarmouth, so that's where I go.

The bank of sites the lady in the office gives me to choose from are not remotely level. Not only am I not sure how you'd put a camper on some of them, I'm not sure how you'd pitch a tent either. But I eventually get set up—and I'm more exhausted than I have a right to be. Maybe it's just the driving in new places that's stressful, even when things go fine.

The bathrooms are pretty sketchy, probably because they're rarely used. This is clearly a seasonal campground, filled with campers permanently moored. For many people, this is a much more affordable option to have a vacation spot in a desirable location than finding a piece of property in their price range. In the three days I'll spend in Yarmouth, I won't encounter another person in this campground. Part of the fun of camping is encountering people walking their dogs on the roads, or nodding in awkward acknowledgment that it's a lovely morning when your mouth is full of toothpaste. It's a particular form of camaraderie and I've been missing these small encounters in a campground.

I put my dinner in the Crock-Pot and go cemetery hunting as the late afternoon sun hangs onto its warmth.

———

IT WAS 1767. PIERRE BABIN[6] AND JOSEPH BABIN AND Pierre Surette[6] had been released from prison and were making plans to move to Yarmouth from Halifax. This is the place where the family would set down roots next to tidal rivers that push and pull with the day, another landscape of uncertainty, of people trying to figure out just what life looks like from here.

The American War for Independence was still several years away, but wars always simmer before they spill over. I can't imagine what it must have been like in those early Yarmouth years, and I wonder what stories they told their children about *le Grand Dérangement*, the years in the woods, prison, and what to do if the British come for them again, how they would prepare for a British victory against the Americans, or what a British defeat would mean for them. Those early years in Yarmouth couldn't have sat easily. They weren't safe, and I wonder how they constructed their lives against such uncertainty.

I wonder what stories they didn't tell, which ones they couldn't because it was too raw, too painful, still too visceral in a way that they felt every day, in the same way that both of my grandfathers rarely spoke of their war service. Silence was for protection, because often when pain runs that deep, there are no words. I understand that—and respect it. I wonder if Pierre Surette[6] told stories of his friend getting stuck in the tunnel they dug to escape—but nothing of the gnawing fear and hunger and cold, the pain of not knowing where the rest of his family were taken. I return to the question of *when does an event become history* and my suspicion that the answer is *when we don't feel it in our bodies anymore*, and I wonder how many generations it took for that time to move from the guts into the bones. I wonder about those I can't find, like Cécile[6]; I know nothing of her other than her birth, and I wonder where and how she died, and how much of what I cannot find is because she is a woman.

I want to know when the misspelling of our name became permanent, from Babin to Babine, though I don't imagine that I'll ever find out when the pronunciation also shifted from *ba-bin* to *bay-byne*. What I'm doing in

Yarmouth feels weightier in a way than what I've done elsewhere, simply because this is the last place they were before
they went to the States. I don't know if there are still relatives here, anybody still living who could be a link to bridge
what's been broken in my family by murder and suicide and
distance. If one of my fundamental questions is *how did
we become who we are*, it seems like the nearly two hundred
years the Babins lived in Yarmouth is part of the answer.

———

IN YARMOUTH ITSELF, I WALK THE CATHOLIC CEMETERY
closest to my campground and try not to get excited by
all the peripheral genealogical names like Surette. While
I find a couple of Babin names not connected to anyone I
recognize, the cemetery proves to be too new to be useful
to me. I've been able to collect data about my great-great-
grandparents Joseph Napoleon Babine[2] and Mary Amero[2]
(Amirault), who were married here in 1876, and three of
their children were born in Yarmouth, but the rest of the
children were born in Massachusetts. I suspect they were
part of the waves of Acadians and French Canadians who
came to these mill towns of the northeast in search of work,
particularly when I find their son's occupation as a *dryer in
a cotton mill*. I'm still in a place where I'm loading dates and
names and places into my brain as pure data, hoping that
my subconscious will put the pieces together in a useful way
once I've accumulated sufficient experiences and knowledge.
I expect—or have faith—that I'll find something here in
Yarmouth, because it's the last place the Babines were before
immigration, but I'm not quite sure where to start looking—
so I start with the cemeteries.

I've spent a lot of time in census records and passenger manifests, trying to figure out when they left, why, and what they did when they got where they were going, because the cause and effect of movement seems to be important in ways I can't yet articulate. In 1871, the Canadian census lists Joseph[2] and his brothers as ship's carpenters, and I want to make connections to the shipyards in Yarmouth, how the Babins became fishermen when they settled in Yarmouth, but it's all speculation. In the 1900 American census, the family is at work in Essex, Massachusetts: Joseph[2], age forty-four, is a carpenter; his oldest son, James, is a farm laborer; his next son, Mandy, is a dryer in a cotton mill, and I don't know what it is about the information contained in census records that is so thrilling. Maybe being able to flesh out people reduced to lines about whether or not they can read and write, what their primary language is, whether they own or rent their home. It's the best work of the family historian, collecting these kinds of documents into the archives, saving the images I find, putting them in their correct folder on my computer, adding necessary information to my genealogy program.

I look at the data the government considers important enough to gather, and I wonder what the government did with the information, gathering all this shiny new data into little boxes they could pull out later. Maybe they didn't know exactly what they'd do with all the information, why it would be necessary to ask a woman how many children she has borne, and how many children she had who were still living. Were they tracking fertility? Infant and child mortality? It's interesting to watch the answers to *Can Read and Write?* go from *no* to *yes* in the course of a couple of decades. First language, French? First language, now

English. In all my census explorations, I still think my Irish great-great-aunt's occupation as a *bow maker, corset factory* is among my favorite details, with her mother occupied as a laundress in the same place, and I note that her father had passed away the year before, likely necessitating everyone in the family to get jobs, and it's a moment when I feel I can restore humanity to dry data.

Maybe it's just that with progress marching on, I'm not prepared for the postdeportation Babines to be elusive. I know that Joseph Olivier Babin[5] was a toddler when the Acadians made their way from Halifax to Yarmouth in 1767, and we have Michel Casimir Babin[4], Benoit Olivier Babin[3], and Joseph Napoleon Babine[2] to sift through before we get to my great-grandfather, but the records of their lives are not easily found, and I did not expect that. Every time I think I'm finding a story, starting to stitch together the tale of who we used to be, the narrative shifts into something else, slides right out of my hands, and all that's left is the accumulation.

———

IN THE MORNING, I HEAD TOWARD ARGYLE, ONE OF THE place-names in my records, to look for cemeteries, a blind searching that's its own kind of delight, hoping I'll stumble over something, which I don't. There's a certain glee in spotting a cemetery, pulling off the road, and just walking through the lupins to see what's there. It's not raining, but everything is wet, and when the sun comes through, it catches in the blooms of the lupins and illuminates them like a painting, turning something three-dimensional into two dimensions. The vibrant colors don't seem quite real, and it is deeply wonderful. I remember the faded colors of Fundy National Park and my faded mood, and I'm glad the feeling hasn't transferred.

After a morning of tramping through long, wet grass in my polka-dotted rain boots, taking more photographs of lupins than is probably necessary, I come back to Yarmouth proper and spend an hour in the Yarmouth County Museum and Archives. I don't find much of anything and the archivist, who is very nice, says that I might have more luck down the road at the Tusket archives, which is how I find out that Yarmouth is divided between the French and English parts of the county.

She says what I'm looking for will be found in Tusket.

The Argyle Township Courthouse and Archives in Tusket are housed in an old white church, and a very nice young man, who is probably in his late teens, helps me as we start my query. This place holds the municipal records for the district of Argyle. It's been a long time since I've gotten elbow deep in archives without a focused query, and there are few things in the world that are more delightful than this fizz in the blood of having absolutely no expectations, only hope. The last time was the giant church records at Chisago Lake Lutheran Church in Center City, Minnesota, that held all of my Swedish relatives' comings and goings since their immigration in the 1860s. There's such a thrill to matching that handwriting to the stones carved in Swedish just outside. My Swedish is rusty and limited to Christmas cookies and a few children's rhymes, but I learned enough to figure things out. The same is true of French, which I don't speak.

Tusket is another of those moments when I'm constructing the archive, the memory, on my own. It feels good to be
adding to the data, not just taking it and taking credit for it,
and this is part of my developing ethic as the family historian. The construction of the archive, the work of being the
historian, must be active, and I must contribute to it, not
simply stumble onto somebody's tree on Ancestry or other
work done elsewhere and claim it as my own. I must do the
work also—that's my job. And my nerdy joy. It's spending the time in databases, the grunt work, the dusty work
of walking into the historical society in Deadwood, South
Dakota, looking for information on the ancestors there, and
finding my great-grandfather's death record (tuberculosis,
which matches family stories) in a giant handwritten led-
ger, but it's also the joy of handing the archivists a photograph of my great-grandfather in his police chief uniform
and them absolutely losing their minds at his badge on his
chest, because their police department was in the process
of redoing their badges to look like the old ones, but they
didn't have any pictures. The best part of the construction
of the archive is in the give and take.

My great-aunt Katherine will be our historian until her
death in 2016, and my mind likes the pattern of her presence and departure from this life: my nephew Henry was
born on her birthday in 2013 and my nephew Sam will be
born on the day she dies in 2016. I want to believe that
the cosmos has order, that it's not just an accident that the
boys' story is intertwined with hers so closely. I like the
patterns, like I'm sliding story stones around until the right
ones touch.

I want the archives to reveal their patterns to me, the
surprise of Michel Casimir Babin[4] sharing a birth date with

Anne Elizabeth Babin, that split second of unrecognition in the same way I looked at the death dates of Walt and Catherine and didn't know what I was looking at—but of course, Michel and Anne are twins, and I want to start looking for the moment I can say *twins run in the family*. There's no pattern to suggest they do, but I wonder about what the body knows in this place that my consciousness does not, if there's room for this spatial memory, if there's even room for my bones to recognize this place in a way my brain does not.

From a scientific standpoint, this isn't particularly far-fetched. We carry the places we've been in our bones, from our teeth recording our childhood geography and diet to every one of our 206 bones. Cells turn over every seven years, and your bones record their own isotope history. We know so much about the life of Ötzi, the Bronze Age mummy discovered in the Alps in 1991, because of the story his bones left behind. Even though we only have forty-seven bones of Lucy, one of the oldest hominid fossils found to date, we know how old she was when she died, how tall she was, and what she ate. The story of Native tribes in the Pacific Northwest is written into the bones of the Kennewick Man, carbon-dated to about nine thousand years ago, and who was finally, after a long legal battle, rightfully returned to the coalition of five Columbia Basin tribes for reburial in 2017. Your bones know where you've been, even if your brain does not. I haven't lived in Minnesota since 2001, when I left after college—and I wonder how much of the place is left in my bones, what a forensic scientist might find in my teeth. Since I carry the DNA of my ancestors, do I carry their places too? If I knew how to look, could I find Yarmouth in my bones? Maybe it's enough that

I carry the Flowerpots, Cabot Beach, and Lunenberg in the memory and history that I'm building for myself right now that nobody else carries. Maybe that's too fanciful, but I like to think so.

━━

MY YOUNG ARCHIVIST FRIEND GIVES ME SOME MARRIAGE records to look through, and I think it's about the third page where I find Joseph Napoleon Babine's marriage to Mary Miro, one of a thousand ways Mary's surname of Amirault is misspelled on various documents, and I know I'm in the right place to find what I'm looking for, if it's to be found. It's a delicious moment, and I think my savage glee makes my new friend a little nervous.

We don't find anything useful in the databases at his fingertips, but then I think for a minute and ask for any church records in the area, particularly Catholic, because the Babines had been Catholic until my grandparents married in 1948, and the Catholics are fanatical about their recordkeeping, which, as a genealogist, I appreciate. In Walt's World War II letters to his mother, he assures her he's going to Mass, even including cards given by the priests at communion as proof of his attendance. My new friend and I hit pay dirt in the parish records of Ste. Anne du Ruisseau, but the irritating stipulation with these records is that I'm not allowed to take pictures of them or scan them, and this is very disappointing. I'm left making sure that I take good notes and can read my own handwriting.

There's a snag when I can't find anything about my great-grandfather. This is weird. He's the most recent of the ancestors to be born in Yarmouth, so Bill Sr. should be here somewhere. I have dates and such pulled from various sources, but I want to see the primary documents, but he's not here. Nothing by any variation of the spelling, so I consider that *if you can't find the answer you're looking for, ask a different question.*

So we start looking by dates.

My young friend wonders, *Because he was French, would he have been baptized Guillaume Henri Babine, not William Henry?*

I say, *It's worth a try.*

The data doesn't come easily, but I find I appreciate the hunt more when it's hard fought, and eventually we find him: a baptismal record for Henri Guillaume Babin. Not Guillaume Henri or William Henry, but the dates match up right.

We found him.

Hello, Great-Grandpa Bill.

I'm able to trace back and back, filling in names and birth dates and siblings and places, and I'm suddenly not as irritated that I can't just scan these records. The zing in my blood is incredible. The act of physically writing them into my notebook, the feel of the pen on the page, the arrows and lines connecting one person to another, the rudimentary family tree sketches to keep track of who's related to who and how, it becomes satisfying in a way that I didn't expect, the physical construction of the documents I'm adding to the story, the work of my very place-specific memory and the knowledge in pages I hold. While the discovery matters, being able to find the lines in their original form matters, I start to wonder if it is the physical act of writing them myself that matters more. Each scratch of the pen on the page, each line drawn to another person, the straight edge of the generations, vertical lines to the next generation, names, birth dates and places, death dates and places—because these people exist spatially on this page, they now exist in my memory in a way that can easily be accessed. Once I've written them down, each time I trans- fer them to a new page, I can recall them as easily as if the data is pulled up in front of me. I don't remember them so much as see them in their place on the page, and I can trace the line back to Antoine[9] and Marie[9] Babin almost without thinking—because I see it. The memory itself is physical, because it exists spatially.

I assume that because these are their church records, they would be buried at Ste. Anne du Ruisseau, but the senior archivist, Peter, tells me not to get my hopes up. He has a warm, open face and a grandfatherly charm, and he seems openly amused by me. I instantly want to be friends. His background is in English, like mine, not history, and I wonder about how many paths there are into the archives.

The Acadians liked wooden crosses for their graves, he says, *so while they're most likely buried there, the graves probably won't be marked.*

He says, *All the families in this area, except for one, spent time after deportation in Massachusetts and then came back here. Those families could come back easier, in the way the Loui- siana Cajuns, or the ones sent elsewhere, could not.*

This makes sense to me, but at this time, I don't yet know about the deportation of Joseph[7] and Anne Marie[7] and their children, the separation from Pierre[6] and Joseph. I don't know that Peter's information about the Babins isn't completely accurate. At the moment, I'm operat- ing under the assumption that that Babins were deported and snuck back in a few decades later. I leave the archives, giddy with discovery, the breadcrumbs of research that are never enough on their own but are enough to lead to the next thing. Rarely will we find a stone cross the size of the Grosse Île memorial to point us where we need to be.

High on details, even incomplete ones, I head for Ste. Anne du Ruisseau, an imposing white church trimmed in black alongside a tidal river, the kind that always balances on the edge of anxiety for me. At high tide, the water rims the shore, but never overflows, even though it always looks like it will. I start with the graves at the back of the church, and like Peter said, there were very few stone markers, and none of them are Babins. On the other side of the road, the cemetery proper, I start with the oldest section and start walking rows, which have a lot of empty spaces where I imagine the wooden crosses Peter mentioned would have marked the graves.

But here's the moment that matters: Grosse Île taught me how to read cemeteries, the way the land dips and waves, and I'm seeing the same landscape pattern here too. I'm looking for dips and waves and I see them.

They're here.

I breathe deeply.

I know how to read this place.

I soon finish this section without finding a single family name. I'm not exactly disappointed, which surprises me.

I know they're here—Joseph Olivier dit Carino Babin[5], who first settled on what would be called Surette's Island. What I will find out later from the Surette's Island group on Facebook is that Carino is an area of Morris Island that was settled by some folk from Eel Brook and it became the nickname of those who lived there. In George Stayley Brown's *Yarmouth, Nova Scotia: A Sequel to Campbell's*

History, he lists the genealogy of several of the establishing families, and there are several to whom Carino is appended in parentheses. The notation reads: *The (Carino) lived in the south of Ste. Anne du Ruisseau called (Flee Town). Two of his sons, Joseph and Jean Henri, lived on Rocco Point. The (Carino) family then went to live on the end of Morris Island, that is still known as the carino [sic]*—and I won't know it was a place until long after I leave. Strangely, this does not feel like failure, and I don't know why. His wife, Elisabeth LeBlanc, was born in Eel Brook, and they're both buried at Ste. Anne du Ruisseau, somewhere. There's an old map I once saw of Morris Island from the 1860s on the Surette Island's Facebook group, and it lists "three white families" on the Carino, to which one of the comments observed that those families would "obviously" be LeBlancs, whose name translates to *white*. There were Black Nova Scotians, but that's not what I think is happening here.

Town names of Eel Brook and Argyle and Glenwood and Amirault's Hill are where the names on the tree start to get musical, away from all the boys named Pierre and the daughters named Marie. This is where the tree starts to sprout Scholastique[4], Julienne[3], Victoire[4]. According to "An Acadian Parish Reborn," which is a fascinating joint digital project between the Nova Scotia Archives and the Argyle Township Court House and Archives:

> With so many people bearing the same or similar first names, it is not surprising that the Acadian population was quick to adopt nicknames as a preferable way of identifying each other. In the earliest parish registers, for instance, there were enough "Joseph Babins" in the local population that the priest, struggling to differentiate among them, described one as "Joseph

Babin dit Nadeau," and others as Joseph Babin "the elder"
and Joseph Babin "the younger." This tradition has persisted
into modern times in the Acadian communities of Argyle.

This explains why so many records have my male ancestors called by their more unique middle names, rather than
their common first names, and I wonder if the same was
true of all the women. I wonder if Joseph[5] was called the
Carino to differentiate him from his uncle Joseph Babin,
who was called l'Ancien. The elder. We have reached a place
where the family was allowed to become old, to become
elders, the carriers of their own history, and that is a gift
in itself.

We've regained a place where we can accumulate memories again in a way that can be told.

CHAPTER THIRTEEN

TODAY I AM IN SEARCH OF FOSSILIZED WATER, YET what I am finding is everything but. It is a dense morning here on the Blue Beach of Nova Scotia, on the western edge of the peninsula on the Bay of Fundy, near Grand-Pré, almost claustrophobic in the low clouds and threats of rain. It is a day of indefinable unease, not one thing or another, the kind of day that puts your blood on alert without really knowing why. Maybe it is the press of wet trees in Longfellow's forests primeval, dripping down my neck without warning, a sharp startle as I walk the path to the beach. As I again bless my camping foresight to bring rain boots, I avoid the most insistent of thick mud puddles as I gingerly make my way from the Blue Beach Fossil Museum to the bay, my head filled with paleontology and geology and a little bit of Indiana Jones searching for the Holy Grail.

The cats and I left Yarmouth yesterday under a very low cloud ceiling. It was a gorgeous drive along the western edge of the peninsula, strangely more so than the eastern Atlantic drive to Yarmouth on the 103 a few days ago. I don't know how to account for it, but it *feels good* to be here. I'm coming to understand the particular gravity of the Bay of Fundy; it's getting into my bones. There are places on the planet that hold more gravity, and this is one of them.

Rick Bass once wrote:

Once they get into you, they are as jealous as a lover; they will never let you look at other mountains again, and you will never want to. When you are away from them, they will be all you think about. Weeks, months, even years will be measured in terms of how long you've been away, and how long it is till you return.

I'm starting to understand that there's something about this place, this water, these forests primeval, that I'm never going to be able to escape. I wonder what my bones will say in twenty years about these days in Acadie.

The tide is out, the distinctive red of silt stretching until I can barely see water. The sky may have been the blue-gray of the rain clouds that have dogged me since Halifax, but the Bay of Fundy is always red. There is a part of me that enjoys the consistency, as if the bay maintains its own character in the face of the largest tides in the world. I am not alone on the beach looking for fossils that would explain how we came to evolve from creatures of the primordial ooze into creatures with fully formed vertebrae and four legs, but I might as well have been. I'm here for nothing but the sake of curiosity, because of a paleontological conundrum called Romer's Gap.

———

ON MAY 17, 1917, SELECTIVE SERVICE PASSED THE UNITED States Congress, establishing the draft of all the eligible men, regardless of citizenship status. William Henry Babine Sr., born in Nova Scotia, was living in Massachusetts and drafted on May 24, according to his naturalization papers. He was twenty-eight and unmarried. He had immigrated to the United States in 1892 through the port of Boston at the age of three, though passenger manifests list the family going back and forth to Yarmouth frequently. His papers, yellowed in the scans online, list him as five feet nine and three-quarter inches tall, with a dark complexion, brown eyes, and dark hair. He would pass this resemblance down to his twin sons, then to all five of his elder son's children. The photographs of my father, grandfather, and great-grandfather at the same age are a stunning experience in genetics.

Bill was assigned to the Army Quartermaster Corps and sent to Camp MacArthur, Texas, for training, and between his naturalization papers, his discharge papers, and other archival information I have uncovered, there is a four-month gap in his records I cannot account for, and this gap seems very, very important.

What I want to know is if Bill went to France.

He was honorably discharged at the end of the war, became a naturalized citizen, and married Catherine in 1922; they promptly moved from Maine to Long Beach, California. The threads here are so thin, the reaching so hard, but the wanting is intense, because if I'm questioning the multiple Great Upheavals in the Babine line and how they led to the current fragmented construction of the family, I think that Bill Sr.'s service in World War I is one of the most pivotal, one of the most important moments that shifted how the family functions. But the reality is that nothing will change if I never know, because nothing will have changed, so disappointment isn't even a factor. Maybe you can miss something you never had, but I'm not sure that's true here. *I want to know if Bill went to France,* because there's a clear Before and After in these four months, and I want to explain the cross-country move, his alcoholism, what feels to me like self-medicating for PTSD, which would not become an official diagnosis for many more years. I want to know if his blood recognized something on the ground in Europe, if something in his bones recognized the weight of the air.

I wonder if he was sent to France because he spoke French, if he became valuable as a translator, and I wonder if he muttered to himself in French when he was drunk, stumbling around the yard with a bottle in his hand while Catherine and the boys kept their distance, war so loud in his head that the darkness of that back shed was the only place the world quieted enough for him.

I don't know anything about war, but I know about fear. My dad was attached to Grand Forks Air Force Base for most of my life, and the only real thing I knew as a child about Grand Forks was the missiles spread out over North Dakota and the heat of the Cold War in the 1980s and that if Russia launched nukes at us they'd aim for Grand Forks. For a small child with no concept of war, of death, the terror I felt every time my dad left for his weekends or his annual tour wasn't anything I could put into words. When the First Gulf War started with Operation Desert Storm in January 1991, Kristi, Kim, and I discussed plans to tie Dad up and hide him in a closet if he got called up. They were elaborate plans. Their first fears about Dad and war didn't happen until then, when Kristi was nine and Kim was seven. Mine came much earlier.

We learned about war in school, but the knowledge wasn't real. Like other parts of my knowing, it felt like

Monopoly money, tangible but not real. I remember standing at Gettysburg, though, on one of our family camping trips, wondering if I would see any of the ghosts of the First Minnesota Infantry Regiment, who had helped lead the Union to victory, and who had also captured the Virginia battle flag. To this day, Virginia wants it back, and Minnesota refuses every time, and I love the pettiness of it. Two of my three-greats grandfathers on my mother's Swedish side fought in the Civil War, but I know next to nothing about their service except a tiny trickle of a thread that might place Charles Shoberg in Chattanooga, where I live now, after the Battle of Missionary Ridge. Charles would have been sent home to southern Minnesota in time to quell the Dakota War of 1862, which resulted in what remains the largest mass execution in United States history, before joining Sherman on his March to the Sea.

There's no such thing as being on the right side of history when it comes to war, because idealism doesn't cancel out the abject cruelty of what humans will do to each other if someone gives them permission, tells them that the enemy deserves what's coming to them, justifies the superiority of the cause. *War is hell*, and Sherman wasn't wrong. The problem with hellfire is that the smoke gets into your lungs and goes home with you. I have no way of knowing if Bill Sr. went to France and came home with mustard gas in his lungs, the sound of bombs in his ears, an unmooring of himself from the ground where he stood, the people who loved him best. I don't know, but I wonder, and then I wonder if I look just a little harder—if I wonder just a little bit longer—if I might be able to fill this gap of knowledge and understand his suicide, or how the legacy of this trauma might have influenced who his sons grew up to be. There are consequences to the unknowing for this family, and they've trickled down into generations I can touch.

These are the generations close to me. For most of this trip, the ancestors have been very ancestral, paper-thin, translucent enough to see through. They belong to history, not to me, and I start to think that here is where the collective history of the Babines starts to become individual again. Here, as I'm standing on Blue Beach and thinking about my great-grandfather who I never met, or Walt who I never met, but I know people who knew them, loved them well. That's close enough to mean something.

———

The Blue Beach Fossil Museum is definitely a mom-and-pop operation, not exactly a proper museum. I don't catch half of what the owner tells me about his collections laid out in front of me, but the crux is this: in our history, there's the time when we're in the primordial ooze, and there's the time when we're walking on land and there are fossils from the ooze, fossils from the land, but there are no fossils from that transitory period that would show scientists how we came to have our backbones and legs. Tangible proof or our ability to move differently, of strength and stability.

The first scientist to theorize about this was a Harvard scientist in the 1950s named Alfred Sherwood Romer, and we're still in search of those fossils to prove his idea. If there are fossils from this period, they're either somewhere in Scotland or here at Blue Beach. Nobody's found them yet, but Romer's Gap is shrinking. While something about that is satisfying, I also find myself hoping that some mysteries of the world and how we came to be who we are remain. Always one more thing to look for, to search, to hope for. The work of science, the work of the family historian, is the same: the impact is in the movement, not the acquisition of the thing itself.

The owner tells me that to find fossils, you have to turn over the rocks on the beach, because the imprints will be made on the mud that settled into the space left by decomposing plants or animals. They won't be facing up. When I go down to the beach and start turning over rocks, I'm not looking for anything specific, though I hope to find ripple marks—which I do. He is right: it's back-irritating work. Not backbreaking, but my spine is clearly miffed when I pause. I'm pretty excited about taking home fossilized water, though, or at least evidence of its movement, as it reminds me of the marks the ice age Missoula Floods left on the landscape of the Pacific Northwest. I'm not looking for the missing fossils of Romer's Gap, or really even any specific fossils, or footprints, or anything that might be exciting to more than me. At the moment, I'm just enjoying the part of me that never outgrew collecting rocks. A few people out on the mudflats seem a lot more hardcore about their digging than I am, and there's a part of me that envies them their dedication to whatever they're looking for.

I love ancient landscapes, erosion that can only be measured in thousands of years and quarter inches. I wonder about seeing the same view my ancestors did three hundred years ago, and I absolutely do not care about the cliché of it. I wonder if this place, not far from where they lived, formed their teeth, their bones, in a way that I could inherit. If I pull the lens back, can I see the movement of people making a home in this place? Land that had been stolen from the Mi'kmaq, then stolen from the Acadians, from Joseph[7] and Anne Marie[7] and Joseph's brothers, those I know for sure were loaded on ships without much time to gather more than they could carry and dumped wherever the ship happened to be pointed. The British were good at dumping people and not caring if they survived. I wonder about the British planters brought in and given their land, what they thought when they walked into the Babin family home and found all their possessions still there, and I wonder if they made a life at Anne Marie's table with her soup pots, in Joseph and Anne Marie's bed. I suspect so.

———

I WANT TO KNOW IF BILL WENT TO FRANCE.

The evidence I have is compelling, and it sizzles in my blood, the way that data points layer on top of each other, sketch out the shadows of a story: the date on his naturalization papers is the last day troop transports left Hoboken for France. Census records say his first language was French, and I imagine his parents still spoke French at home, though they would have been fluent in English as well. On Bill's discharge papers, a stamp reads *approved for the Victory medal,* which Google tells me was only given to those on the ground in Europe. My Swedish great-grandfather, who was also drafted but never left the States, never received one.

The truth is this: I will never know. The records are gone, reduced to ash. Strangely, the loss of Bill Sr.'s records does not bother me, even though I would have loved to see them. If the records are gone, and all that is left is silence, that somehow seems right, even respectful. Again, my search for a thread becomes the thread itself, a story that keeps eluding me not a failure but instead the story itself.

———

My friend Jim once told me that silence is not always a failure, that we need to respect the choice to stay silent where it exists in a story.

Mark Doty once wrote that if there are gaps in memory, let them be part of the telling.

I think the same is true of fragments and the ways that, over time, they add up to a story, even when the story remains elusive over decades or resists being told over centuries. I might not have firsthand knowledge of my grandfather's stories, but my dad does, and my aunt does. My grandfather talked about various things at various times, which have been retold to me in fragments because there's shame and pain and things that aren't suitable dinner conversation, especially when there are young kids at the table. Some of these things are shrouded for good reason. Now I carry many of those stories, their gaps patched with my archival discoveries, and I understand why we don't tell them. Maybe it's enough that I know, that somebody alive always knows.

———

In my hand, I hold my grandfather's World War II draft card. His twin's is next to it.

In October 1942 the boys turned eighteen, and I'm trying to imagine my grandfather as an eighteen-year-old boy, serious and responsible, holding down various jobs that I

imagine kept the family solvent through his father's drinking and the Depression. I remember one story about my
grandfather's job at the local grocery store, labeling canned
vegetables on sale, eight cents each or three for twenty-five
cents, his boss's idea of a joke. I'm imagining that these
were the years when my grandfather was saving up for a
car, which Walt would always want to borrow, which the
stories seem to indicate as evidence that my grandfather was
more responsible than his brother.

But even that is a skewed version of whatever the story
is, whoever the boys were, so I go back to the data to see
if there's any foundation. I'm remembering that the 1920
census lists my great-grandfather's occupation as a chauffeur for a private family in Kennebunk, and my grandfather's draft record in 1942 lists his work as employed by
the Chevrolet Motor Company, and I wonder if Bill tried to
bond with his sons over the magic of engines, the music of
movement from one place to another. I don't know.

What I do know is that when Bill Sr. and Catherine
moved to Long Beach from Kennebunk, Maine in 1922,
the city directories list her as manager for the Belmont
apartments, registered Democrat, and Bill is a glazier for
the American Glass Company, registered Republican. I
come to love city directories that list occupation, as well as
names and addresses. I am strangely charmed by knowing
that both of them were registered voters, particularly Catherine, who in 1922 had only had the right to vote for two
years. I read so much into this tiny line of data—not just
that she's registered to vote, but she's in a relationship that
allows her to be so strong as to vote differently than her
husband, but she was also thirty-two when they married.
She'd been living on her own, living her life on her own

terms, for a long time, and as I'm currently thirty-five, trying to live my life on my own terms, I appreciate Catherine just a little bit more in these moments. When my Minnesota grandparents got married, they came from different party affiliations, but decided they would discuss and vote together, so as not to cancel out the other's vote. Just that tiny letter next to Catherine's name tells me so much that I'd never be able to know another way.

In later years, Catherine is a housewife, raising the twins, still registered Democrat, and Bill Sr. has switched political parties, moving up in the world from glazier to salesman to assistant manager to store manager for Pittsburgh Paint and Glass. There's a break from 1933–1935 when they were in Bakersfield, a gap I can't account for or trace, and then they're back in Long Beach. As the story goes, Bill struggled with cutting the large sheets of safety glass that became more common in cars, which apparently used a different technique than regular glass, and because it was expensive and Bill broke enough of them—a reoccurrence in which his drinking may or may not have been a factor—he either quit or was fired, somewhere around 1938. The family then moved to Ramona in 1939. Catherine is listed as a housewife until after Bill's death in 1943, when she got a job as an accountant for one of the local turkey hatcheries.

The military's Sole Survivor Policy, which I first heard about from *Saving Private Ryan*, would not become law for several more years and could not protect any of the three Babine men being drafted in this moment, even as Catherine faced an empty house in Ramona. I wonder if Catherine ever sat at her kitchen table, late at night, with all her men asleep, holding all three draft cards and facing the very real risk that her entire family could be killed. I wonder if she sat in much the same posture as my seven-greats grand-mother Anne Marie Landry[7], two hundred years before in Acadie, worrying about her husband and sons in that tu-multuous time leading up to the deportations, sitting in the pale of an evening fire by herself, keeping vigil while the house was asleep.

———

ANOTHER GAP:

I have a photograph of my grandfather in his Army uniform, poised to throw a snowball at whoever is holding the camera, a look of deep mischief on his face. He and Walt were fraternal twins, but even as babies, I'd never mis-take one for the other. I hold my grandfather's Bronze Star commendation for bravery at the Battle of the Bulge, trying to comprehend that my grandfather was only twenty years old when he earned it.

For meritorious service in connection with military opera-tions against the enemy in Germany on 21 November 1944. When a telephone line to an observation post was broken, Private First Class Babine volunteered to repair the line which was under constant artillery, mortar, and sniper fire. With complete disregard for his own safety, he succeeded in locating and repairing the break. His action contributed ma-terially to the efficient operation of the company's mission and reflects high credit upon the soldier and the military service.

The story goes that the communications line kept break-ing, and my grandfather volunteered to go back and forth under heavy fire to keep repairing it. In a twenty-four-hour period, even with his efforts, the command post only had three minutes of communication with the observation post, but it seems those three minutes were the right minutes. All I can think in that moment is of what is broken, the lines of communication, what we read in the blank spaces between lines, Romer's Gap everywhere we look. But the other part of the story is that in the darkness, in the cold, my grandfather kept stumbling over rough terrain in the trenches as he went back and forth. In the morning, he found out he'd been tripping over dead bodies. He never wanted to know if they were German or Allied. I don't blame him.

His own father had been dead for a little more than a year. His twin brother was with the Marines in the South Pacific. My own mind has problems comprehending that he was only twenty years old, too young. It's easy to assign deep responsibility to my grandfather, but he had to know the risks when he volunteered to repair the lines. I look at those dates, I look at the citation, and wonder if it was something else. It must have seemed like certain suicide. Maybe a part of him didn't care.

I'll never know what might have happened to Bill Sr. in France, whether the enemy that Bill Sr. faced was the one he saw in the mirror each morning, but maybe I don't need to know.

———

I LEAVE BLUE BEACH WITH THE JEEP LOADED DOWN WITH a ridiculous amount of rock, stored next to my Thunder Bay amethyst, get back on the road, and head to Windsor to see the Fort Edward Historic Site, one of the forts built in Acadian settlements during Father Le Loutre's War and one that played a major role in *le Grand Dérangement*. The name on my records is Pisiguit, which was renamed Windsor after the expulsion, and there's deep satisfaction to putting my tires to places that I've only known through records, through handwritings, through my fingertips. Pierre Babin[6] was born there; his parents, Joseph[7] and Anne Marie[7], were married there. When hostilities began to brew between the British and the Acadians, the British started building fortifications near major Acadian settlements, and Fort Edward was nearest to Pisiguit. Pierre Babin[6] and Joseph Babin, along with Pierre Surette[6], could have been as easily sent to Fort Edward as to Fort Beausejour. When I am there, I know the place is important, but I don't know the full extent of why until later.

The weather has turned decidedly cold, and being so exposed has lost its allure. Maybe the gaps are too large to fill. What's left at Fort Edward is the blockhouse, the oldest in North America, and the incredible earthworks that feel like visible veins under the skin, but the blockhouse, without its full context, is uninteresting. I have no interest in the finer details of its construction or imagining troops in bright red coats in formation on the grass. At the time, I don't know that Pierre Babin[6] and Pierre Surette[6] could have been imprisoned here.

Without knowing what I am looking at, I find myself buffeted by sharp, cold wind, and in this moment, something clicks firmly in my head, and I am no longer interested in trying to reconstruct what is not there.

CHAPTER FOURTEEN

I T'S ONE THING TO STAND ON THE DIKES THE ACADIANS built or to experience the singular sensation of reading *Evangeline* in this place—*in the Acadian land, on the shores of the Basin of Minas, / Distant, secluded, still, the little village of Grand-Pre / Lay in the fruitful valley*—but it's another thing entirely to match the St.-Charles-des-Mines here with the names in my records.

The Babins might have started in Port-Royal, what was renamed Annapolis Royal, as the majority of the Acadian community did, but it wasn't long before the group started to expand and settle elsewhere. Antoine[9] and Marie[9] Babin, the first Babins, married and died in Port / Annapolis Royal, and their son Vincent[8] and his wife Anne Theriot[8] were born there, but by the time their children were born in the 1680s, they were in the Grand-Pré area. Vincent and Anne and the rest of the Babins, they're the ones who had their hands in creating the dikes, breaking the land to farm, and the ones who learned what it was to live and love a land as complex as this one. Vincent and Anne, parents of nine children, were married for thirty-one years before Vincent died in 1718 at the age of fifty-three. Anne outlived him by thirty-three years, died in 1751, and never saw her children and grandchildren ripped from this place, never knew her grandsons, Pierre Babin[6] and Joseph, would be imprisoned at Fort Beauséjour and would flee into the woods to escape the British.

As I drink my tea and stare out the front window of the camper, parked at the Land of Evangeline Campground, mere yards from the Bay of Fundy, only two miles from the Grand-Pré National Historic Site and St.-Charles-des-Mines, texts from the family come through on the campground Wi-Fi. Mom and Dad are packing up their camper to head out to spend time with the California Babines; my grandmother Marion has broken her ankle. She'll be in a rehab facility for a few days while she gets stronger. Kristi, Kim, four-year-old Cora, and I will fly out when I get back to town. Strange and fitting that this seems like it'll be the end to the Nova Scotia trip.

———

DIGBY IS A GOOD CENTRAL LOCATION TO VISIT THE PORT-Royal National Historic Site, a reproduction of the first trading settlement in 1605, and from there I move on to the Fort Anne Historic Site, where I have hopes of locating more information about the Babins and the rest of the Acadians. I know the first Babins were there—I know several of them are buried there—but it's something else entirely to look at the landscape and know that, as clichéd as it sounds, I'm seeing something no Babine has seen for three hundred years. There are no records here, only the place and a cemetery with no markers, something that now feels familiar, and the lack of paper that would tell me who Antoine[9] and Marie Mercier[9] Babin were doesn't feel wrong. *Silence is not always a failure.* The moment doesn't last long. It's cold, and it's rainy, and inside seems a better option.

The museum is thorough, though I now find myself suspicious of park personnel in costume but only half in character. I'm curious now about this style of earthwork fort, the same kind I saw at Fort Edward, molding the land. I can't reconcile why the reproduction and the reconstruction feel vaguely wrong, considering reproduction and reconstruction are what I'm trying to do myself in all of this pursuit of Acadie.

In the cold mist, I go walking through the cemetery to see what Acadians I can find, but the cemetery has been British longer than it has been Acadian. Again, as I suspected, all the wooden crosses have disintegrated, but the earliest of my blood is here. It feels odd to have the Frenchness of the cemetery so overshadowed by the British buried here, especially knowing which Babins are here. I wander, thinking of Marie Mercier Babin[9], born 1645, who married Antoine Babin[9] in 1661 when she was sixteen, a man nearly twenty years her senior, and how she spent the next seventeen years of her life pregnant, bearing eleven children—that I know about. Antoine's buried here at the Garrison Graveyard, and after his death, Marie married Guillaume Lejuge in 1688, because what are you going to do when you're forty-three and have eleven children? You marry another man and within a year start bearing his children.

I don't have a death date for her, but it seems only the best of luck that she didn't die in childbirth, as far as I know, but I look at the very even dates of a child born every other year, then a gap, and I wonder if she miscarried, wonder how many of her children survived to adulthood. I keep imagining how exhausted she must have been by twenty-two, with four children, by thirty with eight children. It's hard not to filter her life through my own twenty-first century values, feeling so angry on her behalf that her whole life was to bear children, and I wonder how the woman herself has been erased. Maybe he was attractive and good to her and she enjoyed their sex life and was one of those women who simply adored being pregnant. It's impossible not to project my own interpretations on the data. Who she was, what she wanted out of life, what she got out of life is as much a clean slate as the lawn here that contains Acadian bones beneath the green.

At the Grand-Pré National Historic Site, which has been a protected UNESCO World Heritage Site since 2012, there isn't much left of the parish of St.-Charles-des-Mines, or the cemetery, which was only discovered by accident about a hundred years ago. The parish registers, or what's left of them, were taken into exile, and the remaining documents are in Iberville Parish, Louisiana. The parish registers give some indication of who might be buried here, but as I learned in Yarmouth, the wooden crosses that had marked their resting places are long gone. The sun is bright in the lupins as I move through the site, the kind of deep sunshine that lights without heat. The site has the feel of a park, wide expanses of green, and it feels good to be here.

It feels like this is the place where we became who we are, where we dug ourselves into this soil and said, *Here. This.* It feels like the shift from Port-Royal to Grand-Pré was the shift from still thinking of ourselves as French to being Acadian. I'm used to finding these moments in time, not locations.

This. Here.

The memorial church was built in 1922, and the stained glass inside bears the stories of waves and boats and families deported—and what a thing to render in such a medium as stained glass, so fragile and so strong, letting the light in and shattering it into a thousand unnameable colors. I take a right turn and walk slowly down the lane that bisects what is likely the Acadian cemetery, with Babin bones in the dust under my feet. The bees buzz around me, the lupins fairly glowing in the sunshine, and in this moment, it is enough.

———

Say it in French: *AH-CAH-DEE.*

I repeat the unfamiliar pronunciation, *ah-cah-DEE,* putting the emphasis in different places than the English *a-CAY-dee-a* I'd been using.

I learn to say it right over a tasting of L'Acadie blanc, sunshine gold, crisp in contrast to the roundness of French vowels, at the Domaine de Grand Pré winery. Later, I listen to BeauSoleil's "Recherche d'Acadie"—"In Search of Acadia"—and *Acadie* is the only French word I recognize as Michael Doucet pulls something true and raw from his fiddle, the minor key clear and keening. Later that afternoon, I stand on the dikes the Acadians built in the seventeenth century, I learn that BeauSoleil takes its name from Joseph Broussard dit Beausoleil, a name not far from *Babin* on the memorial to families deported in Grand-Pré.

Beau soleil.

Beautiful sun, in a minor key.

When I left for Nova Scotia, I knew of some of these places, these locations of family sorrow. But I didn't *know* them with my feet, and I didn't know how far I needed to

227

travel to find where it all started, if such a point was to be found. Standing here alone on the Bay of Fundy turns into a moment when I can watch the timelines of history slide against each other, muddled in what is ancestral family history, contemporary family history, and the future history—legacy—I will create for myself on my own.

The beautiful sun, in a minor key, elusive behind a storm system that has drenched Nova Scotia for the past three days, has finally returned, and it brings with it the kind of glorious joy that can only come after suffering days of bad weather while camping. My campsite is only a hundred yards from the Bay of Fundy and those magnificent tides, that red water that never changes color, no matter the influence of the sky. In moments when I sat inside my camper at my tiny dinette table with a pot of tea, watching the rain out the front window, I wonder about the land moving under my feet here in Acadie that I cannot feel, about the geological harmonic resonance created by the tides in this place that I cannot hear.

There are places on the planet that hold more gravity, and I did not expect the Bay of Fundy to become one of them, and this will become part of the stories I will tell about this trip, about this place, and how that story would only belong to me. This place, this moment, it isn't part of a collective identity—it is mine and only mine. I'm starting to understand that there's something about Acadie, this water, these forests primeval, that I'm never going to be able to escape, and that doesn't seem problematic. It's been four generations since Babines have stood in this place, and it feels important that the place doesn't let me go easily, that there's a restoration in this kind of storytelling, even if it doesn't look like what I intended.

It's been four generations since Babines have stood in this place, four generations since a day, maybe one just like this one, three hundred years ago.

———

GO FIND YOUR FATHER, MY SEVEN-GREATS GRANDMOTHER, Anne Marie Landry[7], tells her eldest, her son, Pierre Babin[6]. She's in her fifties, the mother of five, sturdy, dark haired, strong willed.

Pierre[6] is twenty-five, unmarried, and I imagine him tall and dark and lithe, with a face that I'd be able to recognize as my blood and a quicksilver kind of efficient cleverness about him. He has bigger ambitions than marriage, much to the distress of his mother. I have pictures of my father, grandfather, and great-grandfather at about the same age, and I wonder if Pierre and Joseph share their faces.

Pierre does what he's told and finds his father standing in just this place where I will stand, on the dikes his own great-grandparents built against the sea so they could farm the land. Joseph[7] is quiet, as he often is, pragmatic in the way of understanding the world that is specific to farmers.

Rain's coming in, Joseph says, and Pierre nods, wondering what his father sees in the sky and smells in the air that he does not. *We could use a good, soaking rain.*

The water is thick and red, but the waves still break pure white, then pull back out, push and pull, push and pull. They stand in silence for a while, watching the fishing boats come in as the tide turns, their friends and neighbors. Where his father smells rain, Pierre smells trouble. Pierre wonders if his mother feels the same.

Out of his five children, Joseph worries about Pierre the

most, the one who will work the land but does not feel it in his bones. He's the one who is more comfortable on the water, changeable but predictable, a force that moves the landscape with the tides. And yet, Pierre will be one of two Babins left behind, imprisoned as his parents, siblings, and extended relatives are tossed on a British ship and deported to Maryland. Neither of them know this is one of the last times they will stand together and watch the water that will soon tear the family apart. But maybe Anne Marie knows.

ON MY LAST NIGHT IN GRAND-PRÉ, WHEN THE RAIN HAS cleared to a setting sun so pure that it creates sun dogs, rare in June, I walk the tidal flats looking for rocks. My kindred spirit of a niece has recently taken to collecting rocks—much to the consternation of my sister, who wonders where they'll put them all—and I have already saved for her Thunder Bay amethyst and a perfectly shaped egg of white quartz from Yarmouth. Now, on the tidal flats in Grand-Pré, in hours I am not yet willing to leave, I collect petrified wood from what litters the beach, relics of the forests primeval, the grain of wood so clear I can see growth rings in the stone, time held in my palm in a way that I can count, measure in a tangible form, a history I can physically understand. But the history in the stone in my hand is a dead thing, and it is vaguely wrong.

Two young men in their midtwenties come down the steps to the beach, and I stay long enough to watch them catch the echo of twilight in their kites. *This is the best twenty-five dollars I've ever spent!* I hear one of them say, and I think I can hear the melody of a bow in the wind being drawn across the strings in their hands.

CHAPTER FIFTEEN

THE JUNE DAY I LEAVE ACADIE FOR GOOD DAWNS SPEC-
tacular, the kind of sunshine and early morning blue
skies and sparkles on waves that dreams are made of. Last
night was a short night, partly due to the adrenaline of the
impending ferry ride, but partly due to the headlights in
the campground at midnight. I find out that it was people
trying to set up a tent in the dark, but I ended the night
with several very potent serial killer dreams. The alarm
goes off early, not that I really need it, with the spectacular June morning sunshine—and it's just a great morning
to be alive. I get hitched up, put the cats in their kennels,
clean up Maeve's visceral disagreement with the day's plan,
drive down to the ferry dock, and buy my ticket for the ferry
called the *Princess of Acadia*. We're all ready when we're allowed to board just before 8:00 a.m. I realize as I grab my
backpack and thermos of tea that the cats are making sure
I know there will be hell to pay when they get out. I settle
into the Sea Breeze Lounge with the engines shuddering
beneath me. About halfway through the very smooth voy-
age, I go down to check on the cats and realize it is actually
quieter in the vehicle hold than it was in the passenger area.

It doesn't escape me that I am, in a poor imitation of my ancestors, leaving Acadie via the water. I have various passenger manifests that record the Babines going back and forth from Yarmouth to Boston fairly frequently, so it's hard not to think of them as I am on this ferry. The crossing to Saint John, New Brunswick, will take about three hours; I am headed for Kennebunk, Maine, five-ish hours' drive beyond that. In Kennebunk, I hope to catch the last chapter of the Babines, the last eastward point before the family aimed west.

As we get ready to disembark and drive our vehicles off, I turn the key—and nothing. *Well, shit.* I forgot to disconnect the Scamp from the Jeep, so the fridge drained my Jeep battery. Embarrassing, but I won't make that mistake again. So the guys waving us off the ferry use my jumper cables, get the forklift to give me a jump, and all returns to normal. I don't imagine I'm the first or last to have this problem.

When I get off the ferry, I head south toward Kennebunk. It's about an hour to the border, and there are no problems there with Customs, which is great, because I have never been able to shake the intimidation of the IRS and Customs.

They ask what I'm bringing back, and I tell them about my four bottles of wine because I'm a compulsive rule-follower, and so it doesn't occur to me not to say, *I have two cats and do you need to see their paperwork?* They say no, then ask for my key to look inside the Scamp. They're a little uncomfortable when I tell them the door lock is broken, but I open it for them and stand back after I unlatch it, because nobody wants twitchy Border Patrol officers. I want to explain all about the Old Logging Road and the detour in Ontario, the mosquitoes, the wiggle through the back window, but I do not. *The door is broken* doesn't quite seem to cover it. I get back in the Jeep and wait for them to peek inside. Then they ask to look inside the Jeep. *Sure, no problem.* When they open the back hatch, I think they're looking for firewood.

They ask about it, because they don't see any.

I say, *no, I know better than that.*

They smile and wave me on.

So, onward. I get gas at the next gas station, because the physical memory of Ontario remains strong, and I'll never take a full gas tank for granted again. I'm surprised that it takes me longer than I expect for my brain to go back to thinking in miles rather than kilometers, and I like this odd feeling that Canada will linger a little longer.

———

WHEN CORA WAS TWO, KRISTI, KIM, MIKE, AND I WENT to a Rembrandt exhibit at the Minneapolis Institute of Art. The gallery was packed, hardly any room to move, very little space to get close enough to see the faces rendered in paint so long ago that it was difficult to comprehend. A woman we don't know bustled up to Cora with a look I couldn't quite identify and declared, with great and enthusiastic intensity, *She looks just like that painting over there!* We thanked her, awkwardly, having no idea which painting she was referring to, but we decided there are worse things than a beloved child being compared to a Rembrandt painting. We eventually did recognize Cora's face in *Portrait of a Boy*, painted in the 1650s, about the time that Antoine[9] and Marie[9] Babin were getting settled in Acadie. The woman was right. The child in the painting looked like Cora.

It makes me think about family resemblances, especially across time. I have no way of knowing if the photograph

233

in the family archives labeled *Joseph Napoleon Babine*[2] and *Mary Amero Babine*[2], with *Oliver Babine* and *Amero Father*, is accurate. The print is aged enough that it's possible, but Benoit Olivier Babine[3] died in 1899, and Jacques Amirault[3] died in 1873, so I doubt I'm holding evidence of those generations. The men identified as Oliver and Joseph look to be the same age, while the man labeled Jacques Amirault looks a generation older. A separate photograph labeled *Joseph Napoleon Babine*[2] looks more like his son, beard grizzled, sunbaked, wearing a hat low over his head and a bandanna around his neck, crouched in the same position I recognize from another photograph. I'm fairly sure I'm looking at a photograph of Bill Sr., not his father. In another photograph of Bill's sister Josie, the note says she looks exactly like Walt's daughter Catherine. Later photographs of my great-grandmother Catherine in her forties look exactly like Walt's eldest granddaughter, my cousin Alana, the story in a face that can't be written any other way.

The reality with these old photographs is that everything I hold about the first American chapter of the Babines feels suspect. I have an entire box of Babine photographs that came from my dad's cousin Sarah along with Walt's war letters after I've come home from Nova Scotia, but the archive is emotionally incomplete. We trust photographs in ways that maybe we shouldn't, trust that they hold some kind of inviolable truth when they don't. But these photographs do represent a legacy represented in our genetics, our ability to identify who we belong to, because DNA still feels like an immovable force. I might recognize my face in my sister's children, but I'm never going to have this legacy myself. I'm not upset about it, because this is the life I've chosen, but as I'm holding these photographs, I think of that Rembrandt exhibit and how we don't often print photographs anymore. They're all on our phones. We don't have photo albums, boxes of snapshots, because the images are always accessible. The photographic evidence of our lives has somehow become intensely private in ways that I don't think I understood before. Memories erode, sometimes intentionally, and we don't know what to do with the tangible pieces left behind.

———

IN 1980, WHEN SHE WAS EIGHTY-SEVEN, MY GREAT-grandfather's sister Josie sat down with the Brick Store Museum in Kennebunk and recorded her reminiscences and even though the audio quality on the CD is poor, I can make out most of the conversation. Josie never married, worked as a trained nurse, and I wonder just how much of her life choices were dictated by her father's stroke in 1932 and providing him care until he died two years later and not wanting to leave her mother alone in the midst of the Great Depression. I won't know this interview exists until well after I'm gone from Kennebunk. I'll wish I could have listened to it while I was there. Josie's voice is strong, but it has the cadence of speech from a different time, the phrasings of *in those days*; she starts her sentences with *well, yes*, in a way that I heard my grandmothers use but never my mother's generation. Josie says that the family came to Kennebunk Beach when she was seven or eight, for her father to work on the new Atlantis Hotel as a carpenter, one of the many luxurious hotels being built to house the incredibly wealthy tourists coming to Kennebunk for the season. Not just summer, but The Season. The Atlantis Hotel, the Seaside House, the

Sundial Inn, lovely, fanciful names. None of them exist in that way anymore, but Josie described them as incredibly beautiful, incredibly luxurious. Even though her father was working on the building, they were not allowed inside.

In my mind, I'm seeing the White Sands Hotel from *Anne of Avonlea*. I'm seeing dark and silky Edwardian woodwork, Gibson-girl hair, bright crystal, sumptuous fabrics that gleam in the right light. Sand dunes, seagrass, the kind of light specific to the Eastern seaboard. I'm picturing Glensheen in Duluth and transplanting that splendor to the idle rich of Maine or Boston. I'm imagining the fading glitz of Gilded Age New York society, the conspicuous wealth of the Four Hundred, and the society glamor that would spill over into *Titanic* opulence and the death of quite a few who were the type to summer in Kennebunk Beach. I wonder what wreckwood they found on their sands. Several times in her reminiscences, Josie describes a particular woman as "such a lady," and often refers to *the caste system in those days*.

True blue bloods, Josie says. *They were nice, but you always knew where you stood.*

Josie's reminiscences make sense to me, because census records list Joseph's[2] occupation as a carpenter for most of his life. The way Josie tells the story, the owner of the Atlantis Hotel gave Joseph the shack on the beach, and he could do what he wanted with it, so he built it up into a fine home, which still stands, but it was moved off the beach in the 1940s. As I write this, just last week I watched a massive storm come ashore in Maine and destroy structures that had stood there for more than a century. Even Mainers seemed surprised by its ferocity. *Why did you build so close to the beach, then?* internet strangers demanded, only to be informed that when those houses or shacks or lighthouses were built, the shoreline was more than a mile out, and storms over the last century have systematically pulled the shoreline back out to sea.

I've seen pictures of the old Babine house: it's still a primitive house, with two bedrooms and the floorboards of the second floor comprising the ceiling for the first floor. But I wonder about Bill's carpentry skills, working on the house on the beach with his father, and in the *Biddeford Journal-Tribune* from June 1908, the social pages report that "Joseph Babine is building an addition to his house," an event that I would not have thought rose to the level of newsworthy. In the archives, I have two more photographs: the same house, different locations. The earlier picture, dated 1901, shows the house, a solid two-story with a wraparound porch, the only vertical lines on a beach surrounded by gracefully bent seagrasses. The note from my grandfather indicates that this is the original location of the house on the beach of Kennebunk. Sometime after—the second picture is not dated—the house was moved into town. In the second picture, there's a barn on the right side of the frame, a barn that shows up in another picture in which my great-grandfather is holding two draft horses. The sign on the barn says *Joseph N. Babine and Son, Depot Carriage and Transfer.* My grandfather remembers his father saying that when he was a boy, he could jump off the breakwater and go swimming right in front of the house when the tide was in.

In an email, Grandpa wrote:

You asked about what Dad did. My father was a very skilled craftsman. When he lived in Maine with his parents he did a variety of things. He only went to school through the 6th grade, in fact after he and Mom were married, she taught him Mathematics on Sunday after Church to bring him up to speed. He worked as a fisherman in Maine, he worked in his father's drayage business; and he served an apprenticeship as a carpenter which I believe was about 5–6 years. In fact the first year of that apprenticeship, the only thing he was allowed to do was sharpen the tools. Chisels, saws, and planes. After WW1 he moved to Worcester Mass and was employed as a chauffeur. He had to walk to work and he used to pass Mother as she went to work. She was a book keeper for Sessons Casket Co. and they eventually met formal at a Church gathering. That's all I know. When Dad and Mom came to California he went to work in a glass shop, replacing glass in homes, businesses, and in Autos. He left that job during the 1930s and went to work for Pittsburgh Paint company, and for that job we moved to Bakersfield. We stayed there until 1935, when he was transferred back to Long Beach to open and Manage their new store there. We stayed there until the fall of 1938, when he left the paint company, and we moved to Ramona, Ca. In Ramona dad bought some land and with my brother's and my help we built an adobe house and it is still standing today. He built the garage first and we made it so we could live in it and were there for a couple of years while we constructed the house.

It was one of two times where I asked him for a story about his family and he gave me one. Every other time I asked, he simply changed the subject. When they moved to Ramona, they built that adobe house by hand, just the three of them, with bricks in molds they built themselves, and constructed something that would outlive all of them. My dad last saw the house a few years ago, and he said that it's all still original inside—the owners haven't even replaced the kitchen cabinetry. *Why would they?* I asked, somewhat dismissively. *Everything in that house was handmade, custom; why would they want to replace it with dustboard from a big box store that will disintegrate in a couple of years?*

The Babine Tinkering Gene came down through my grandfather and spread to his five children, who have combined the practical and the beautiful in neat ways. When I was a kid, my uncle Dennis made some of the most beautiful wooden puzzles I'd ever seen—and last week, Sam pulled them from where they were stored under the couch to put them together. For Christmas, Dad made Mom a yarn box of black walnut so smooth and silky that it seemed unnatural, but he is equally proud of the Kleenex box holders he made for his truck out of plexiglass.

For the most part, Dad and I are practical builders, tinkerers, and that's how the two of us remodeled the Scamp so that it was exactly what I wanted. It makes me wonder if my great-grandfather Bill Sr. was the same way, if it's a matter of Depression-era thrift, or the realities of rural life and an absence of stores, or something more creative in nature. Velcro, duct tape, wire ties, heat shrink, seat belts sourced from junkyards, these are standard in my dad's house—and mine. Kristi and Kim admit they are not tinkerers themselves, but maybe they don't have to be, because Dad and I are, though Kristi has a truly deft hand with the duct tape to get just a little more life out of something. Next best thing to the skill is knowing someone who has it. We don't throw away extra screws from projects— we save those too. I learned to rewire a lamp in shop class, and it's one of my most useful skills. The summer Dad and I took out the Scamp's stove I never used and fixed the silverware drawer that didn't want to slide, we contemplated

L-brackets and drawer slides before I finally suggested we just cut a new piece of wood to replace the warped particleboard that had gotten wet and swelled, which is what we ended up doing. Simple. Then I wanted to make a flush countertop—which, in my imagination, involved using a cookie sheet to cover the hole, because that was the cheapest way I figured we could get sheet metal that would do the job.

I walked into Dad's shop where he was working on something, showed him my newly thrifted cookie sheet.

He looked up from his project, nodded. *Yeah*, he said. *I think that'll work.* He handed me the anvil and ball-peen hammer without a word and went back to his task. I remind him that there are only two rules of Babine projects:

Rule 1: No Blood.
Rule 2: All Participants Must Be Speaking To Each Other at the End of Said Project.

It's a fair bet that both of us will break Rule 1. We both have tissue paper for skin.

Mom lays down money on Dad breaking first.

That's a sucker's bet.

After I'd pounded it flat and realized it was exactly the size I needed, he handed me the permanent marker and told me to measure to find where the holes should go that would line up with the fiberglass under it.

I did not measure. I eyeballed it.

I did not tell him this.

I walked back into the shop with my cookie sheet.

Are you happy with it? he asked without looking up.

He handed me the punch and I whacked dents in the cookie sheet for us to drill through. Back in the camper, he handled the drill and my non-measurements worked perfectly. A little later, I asked him, had this been his camper, how he would have solved the stove hole / counter situation. The best thing about how my dad and I work together is that we come at problems from very different angles.

Oh, probably the same as you did, he said.

I shook my head. *I mean, what would you have done to cover the hole in the fiberglass? I don't think you would have looked for a cookie sheet.*

No, you're right, he said.

I was just thinking about how to source sheet metal for super cheap.

Yeah, he said, laughing. *I'd probably have done it the most complicated way possible.*

This is true, I agreed.

After time away from my parents' home, there's something deeply satisfying about walking into my dad's shop, seeing the Skippy jars full of bolts and screws on his shelves and feeling absolutely at home, like I know exactly how to find the tools I need to build—or fix—what I want, like everything I need to know about how to navigate the world can be found there.

I wonder about building with my dad, my father and his brothers building with their father, Grandpa and Walt building with Bill Sr., and so on up the family tree, and I wonder just how working with their hands built their relationships—or didn't. I wonder if building with his hands helped curb Bill Sr.'s PTSD, at least for a time, and I wonder about Joseph[2] passing down the Babine Tinkering Gene to my great-grandfather, who passed it down to Grandpa, my dad, and me. I wonder if Bill Sr. ever said *let's go make sawdust* to my grandfather and Walt, the way my father will say to me or to his grandkids and take them out

241

to the shop for a project. The Kennebunk house might still hold Babine memories, in the way I believe Glensheen still holds its memories of the Congdons, and even the adobe house in Ramona might still hold the stories of that first generation of California Babines—but I still think about the work of building those relationships.

————

IN THE MORNING, I GO IN SEARCH OF THE HISTORICAL society in Kennebunkport. The woman there doesn't seem unhappy to see me, but she's not terribly excited about helping me either. The last name doesn't ring a bell with her, which isn't terribly surprising, given that the family has basically died out. The only piece of information I leave with is that Joseph[2] and Mary[2] are buried at Hope Cemetery in Kennebunk, and it's a little bit jarring to realize that yesterday, I was in the earliest place the Acadian Babines laid footprints here, and today I'll stand in the most recent place they were, before they became California Babines.

Hope Cemetery is in the center of town, she tells me. *You can't miss it.*

What the historian neglected to tell me is that Hope Cemetery is immense, one of the largest cemeteries I've seen on my travels so far. The good news is that there are thousands of stones—no wooden crosses here—but this will be like a needle in a stone haystack. No map or directory, so if I want to find Joseph and Mary, I'm going to have to wander. This is a long shot, but it's a beautiful day and I have nothing else to do.

Joseph died in 1934, and Mary died in 1950, so I try to find the burials in the 1930s and see if anything turns up. It takes on the quality of a treasure hunt, which is more delightful than I expect it to be. Joseph was a carpenter—something my pastor's kid history laughed at, especially since his wife's name was Mary—and having no actual idea where to find their stones, I use Indiana Jones Holy Grail Logic (the Grail would be the carpenter's cup, not gold): Joseph and Mary wouldn't have had an expensive stone. He was a carpenter, like his Biblical namesake, not a banker. There aren't many Babines buried here, not a clan, so no family plot, so I can skip those. I figure it'll probably be the simplest of stones.

I haven't wandered twenty minutes when I find them.

I found them.

I can't believe I found them.

I'm right about the stone, fairly low to the ground, simple. I can't believe it. *BABINE,* it reads, with *Mary F.* and her birth and death dates to the left, *Joseph N.* to the right with his dates, and I know that she's Mary Phorienne, not an *F,* and I've never encountered that name anywhere else, so I wonder what significance the name held for her mother. The outer rim of the gravestone is gray, the inner rectangle with their dates much more reddish in hue. It's covered with pale green lichen, moss, a contrast to the much darker stone.

There they are.

Hello.

I just stare at them for a few minutes, in shock, in silence. *I cannot believe I actually found them.* Then I call my dad, who's arrived in California to see his mother and support his father.

Dad puts Grandpa on speakerphone and the three of us just stand over the graves of his grandparents, having a moment.

243

My grandfather says nothing.
Tell me anything.
It doesn't matter what it is.
Tell me something.
He doesn't.

━━━

AFTER I LEAVE THE CEMETERY, I GO WANDERING. IT'S A splendid day for wandering. Looking back, I'll wish I had seen the beach, walked the promenade, gathered some rocks, and came to know with my feet the distance between Kennebunk Beach and Kennebunkport, but maybe it is fitting somehow that I do not.

In the end, though, I buy a cookbook of local Down East recipes, eager to revisit the flavors of this place and its memories long after I leave, and then I go to a pottery shop and consider myself lucky that I escape with only a little pitcher pressed with flowers and ferns and only the smallest of dents in my wallet. I hold this moment in both hands, brimming full of fossil imprints from Blue Beach and Romer's Gap and silences and stories and Fort Edward's earthworks and the landshape of Acadian cemeteries, and I decide there is something particularly nice about taking home an imprint, the shape left by something, rather than the thing itself.

CHAPTER SIXTEEN

THIS IS MY FATHER'S COUNTRY, THIS CALIFORNIA. HE comes from these golden hills, this water, this light. It flows in his veins. He's lived in Minnesota for more than half his life, and he always says he has no desire or intention of returning, but I can't see that as accurate all the time. How could he not desire—at least sometimes—what he left behind for love?

On the airporter from San Francisco to my grandparents' house mere days after I return to Minneapolis from Nova Scotia, I watch the road. Nothing says California more clearly to me than the bumpy lane lines on the freeway that click when you drive over them. Such a novelty to a Minnesotan, who knows that while things like this work here, you put those on a Minnesotan road and they'll get popped up by the first snowplow. I love the gold hills here, the green of scrub oak. The trees are so different from my Minnesota Northwoods, so different from Acadie's forests primeval, but they attract me—I don't have names for them, but I want to climb them. I love the liquid vowels of the place-names—Novato, Santa Rosa, Petaluma, San Rafael—and I want to wear them like rain. We drive north, and I'm seduced by the curve of roof tiles, the earth colors of the missions.

California feels an attitude unto itself as we pass exits with names I recognize from previous visits or my dad's stories. My grandfather once said it's the salt air, but that's not it. California, I think, at its root, is a way of moving. By foot, car, train, cable car. Movement is the reason California exists. If immigrants weren't looking for something else, something different, something better, looking out from the East in the most logical direction—West—then they wouldn't have ended up in California. I wonder what the point was where Catherine looked at Bill Sr., or Bill looked at Catherine, and said, *California.* The idea is complicated and colonizing, but it didn't matter if they were looking for gold or freedom or land or some combination of all of that—the allure of California, as a concept, seems to be the result of all the ways of getting there, across land that was not theirs to cross. Foot, horse, covered wagon, train. Model A sedan. Airplane. There's such optimism in movement, in the allure of elsewhere.

I remember Grandpa's Mustang the best, a glorious '67 Mustang, cherry red. Every time Dad rode in it with Grandpa, he came back sunburned the same red color as the car but happy. Grandpa rarely let him drive it. Any time we're on California roads, Dad points out cars next to us on the highway that we thought only existed in dreams and songs out of the '60s. Lamborghini. Dodge Viper. Shelby Mustang. Where's *the little old lady from Pasadena*? Nobody writes songs about Minnesota.

Joan Didion writes in *The White Album*:

> To understand what was going on it is perhaps necessary
> to have participated in the freeway experience, which is the

only secular communion Los Angeles has. Mere driving on the freeway is in no way the same as participating in it. Anyone can "drive" on the freeway . . . Actual participants think only about where they are. Actual participation requires a total surrender, a concentration so intense as to seem a kind of narcosis, a rapture-of-the-freeway. The mind goes clean. The rhythm takes over.

This is a communion I don't understand as one who grew up in rural northern Minnesota, who was afraid to drive the four lanes of Highway 10 into Fargo–Moorhead until college. I am actually capable of driving a stick, but I tend to panic when I'm on an actual road, and then I get stuck at stop signs. Yet this sort of movement in California feels like the bedrock of the way Californians think—or at least I'm seeing this in the California Babines, or at least with my grandfather.

When I arrive at my grandparents' house, I carry my suitcase through the garage, past the laundry room, and into the house, nearly stopped in my tracks by a familiarity of scent, a little soapy, a little powdery, but somehow a little sharp, and it's a smell that spans decades of memory: when I'm here, this smell reminds me of things I know in this place. Once I've settled, I come downstairs and stand at the patio doors, looking out into the garden. The dining room of the California Babine house occupies the formal side of the house, with a lovely view out the side window to my grandfather's prized roses, and past the end of the table, a view out the patio doors to Grandpa's immaculately landscaped backyard, terraced in brick. The carpet is deep, thick burgundy, and it muffles any footfalls. The table is dense, heavy wood, and it has a gravity, too, and matches

the sideboard behind it, topped with a large mirror. All the
light in this part of the house is indirect.

I've just spent five weeks on a journey to the family's
origins to find out how this family came to be where they
are, who they are, but my grandfather will not ask me a
single question about my trip. Not a single curiosity about
what I've found about his family, his ancestry. One afternoon, I sit with Dad and Grandpa on the back patio in the
shade of my grandfather's magnificent garden as the two
of them talk about Grandpa's travels, under the pergola
that his children stained the day his mother and brother
were murdered, now shaded by fifty years of vines. My dad
talks about the trip west, how quickly they set their pace to
get here to see Marion, and how long the days were, about
steep grades and transmissions and places they stopped; my
grandfather talks about engines and taking his little Geo
Tracker up to the lake to go fishing and the fishing pole
holder he made out of PVC. Dad and I grin at him. We
do love a good PVC project, his most recent being an extension of the sump pump discharge out of the side of his
house into a T shape drilled with holes to turn the water
into a sprinkler to water the front garden so the force of the
ejected water doesn't erode a trench in the soil.

*We made the closet in Karen's Scamp out of PVC a few years
ago*, my dad says, and he looks at me.

Recognizing the conversational softball for what it is,
I elaborate. *We used one-inch PVC and created a ladder that
pressed into the closet, because it's thin fiberglass and you can't
screw anything into it. It was actually a pretty easy project, but
it really makes the Scamp more livable.*

Grandpa nods and changes the subject, maybe the nails
he put under his hydrangeas to change the pH of the soil to

change their color. Dad and I look at the flowers, huge and gorgeous and spilling over the brick terrace. They are incredibly beautiful. Dad tries to steer the conversation back to me, back to Nova Scotia, but my grandfather steers it away so deftly that I won't realize what he's done till later. At the time, I wondered how he could be so incurious, but now I simply wonder if the subject of his history, immediate and ancestral, was simply too painful.

So I stare out at the backyard, at the hole where our swing tree used to be, and I feel the memory of the softness of garden hoses that Grandpa put around the chains to protect little hands, the painful scratch of the holly tree against our bare shins when we swung too high. The rosebushes are largely gone now, but in my memory they're taller than I am, every shade of red to pink and peach and some that were two colors, and as a five-year-old I'd never seen rosebushes before, because we can't grow roses at home. Mom loved her flowers and let us pick out whatever ones we wanted for our own flower gardens, the petunias and snapdragons and the sharp scent of marigolds, but not roses. In my memory, I step carefully from one paver to the next behind them on the terrace, hiding behind the roses, five years old, with blonde curls that will darken and straighten as I age.

Later in the afternoon, after the talk under the pergola, I watch Grandpa take four-year-old Cora by the hand and give her the tour of the backyard, the birdbath, showing her each flower by name, a tiny blonde girl in a long-sleeved gray shirt and blue athletic pants that could have been any of the three of us thirty years ago, and from the back, Grandpa could be mistaken for my dad: the same stance, the same gait, the same hair. The genetics are startling, and it makes me smile.

Time dissolves a little, and the accordion of history expands and contracts, and everything about this multi-layered moment is wonderful, gentle in the way of early summer sun.

⸺

THREE YEARS LATER, BOTH GRANDPARENTS ARE GONE, MY grandmother in 2015 and my grandfather in 2017, and I hear my grandfather's voice in my father's recollection, that he wouldn't go back to visit his parents' or brother's graves, *because if he didn't tell them he loved them in life, it made no sense to say it now*, and I've collected their gravestones into my memories, for my archival records, too, because their active creation of the family story has ended.

That summer, Cora and I go camping north of Duluth, and we go hunting on the shores of Lake Superior for stones. *We're going to make story stones*, I say, picking up one, then discarding it for a thinner, smoother specimen, showing her what we're looking for. The stones themselves are largely gray-blue granite, porous, and they will soak up the paint she uses to draw. I should have packed acrylic. Cora's ore boat looks like a caterpillar, but we know what it is. She paints waves for water on one stone, a bright sun on another, a cloud on another, then a campfire. She draws the cascades of Gooseberry Falls. I paint the Scamp, and it's decently recognizable. Cora hands two stones to me and directs me to draw Split Rock Lighthouse with a beacon of lightning from its eye, even though it's only lit once a year on the anniversary of the *Edmund Fitzgerald*'s sinking, and I think about direction, illumination, and how all stories are fragments, reconstruction. When we return home, she sets the stones on the coffee table in front of her parents, shifting the fragments of story to tell the tale of who she is and where she's been in whichever way she chooses.

Notes

xvii   ***There is a pull*** W. Scott Olsen, "Gravity" from *Gravity: The Allure of Distance*, (University of Utah Press, 2003).

23   **When you begin a road trip** Olsen, "Pointed Home - 1991" from *Gravity*.

62   **There is no credit** *The Shadow*, radio broadcast, performed by Orson Welles, March 13, 1938, 25:50, https://www.youtube.com/watch?v=fDnIzVKe1cE.

63   **And away to the northward** Henry Wadsworth Longfellow, "Part the First - I" in *Evangeline: A Tale of Acadi*e, https://www.hwlongfellow.org/poems _poem.php?pid=269.

75   **Solitude is not something** Thomas Merton, "Entering" in *The New Man*, reissue ed. (New York: Farrar, Straus and Giroux, 1999).

78   ***a 2021 article*** Susan Molinari and Beth Brooke, "Women are more likely to die or be injured in car crashes. There's a simple reason why." *Washington Post*, December 21, 2021, https:// www.washingtonpost.com/opinions/2021/12/21 /female-crash-test-dummies-nhtsa/.

83   *discarded early draft* Paul Gruchow, *Boundary
Waters: The Grace of the Wild* (Minneapolis:
Milkweed, 1999), 190.

96   *There is too much controversy* "Catherine
LeJeune," Find a Grave, added January 22, 2014,
https://www.findagrave.com/memorial/123968483
/catherine-lejeune.

121   *this, coupled with thousands* Rudy R. Frame Jr.
"Okinawa: The Final Great Battle of World War
II," *Marine Corps Gazette*, October 2012.

149   *When a sixteen-year-old* John Yang, "Florida
Judges Rule Teenage Girl Is Not Mature Enough
to Have an Abortion," PBS News Hour, August
19, 2022, https://www.pbs.org/newshour/show
/florida-judges-rule-teenage-girl-is-not-mature
-enough-to-have-an-abortion.

150   **injurious relating on the grossly** Margaret
Crastnopol, *Micro-trauma: A Psychoanalytic
Understanding of Cumulative Psychic Injury* (New
York: Routledge, 2015), 1–2.

166   **I like fossicking** Tim Robinson, *Listening to the
Wind* (Minneapolis: Milkweed, 2019), 89.

176   **the thing I came for** Adrienne Rich, "Diving
into the Wreck" from *Diving into the Wreck: Poems
1971-1972* (W. W. Norton, 1973).

182   **the thing I came for** Rich, "Diving into the Wreck."

183   **July 23 1755** Clarence J. d'Entremont, "The First
Expulsion of the Acadians of Southern Nova

Scotia—1756," Acadian.org, www.acadian.org
/history/first-expulsion-acadians-southern-nova
-scotia-1756.

184   **In 1755** Clarence J. d'Entremont, "The Siege of
Fort Beauséjour," Acadian.org, https://www
.acadian.org/history/siege-fort-beausejour.

184   **I hold this (information)** D'Entremont, "The
Siege of Beauséjour," Acadian.org.

186   ***after two years of misery*** D'Entremont, "The Siege
of Beauséjour," Acadian.org.

187   **the thing I came for** Rich, "Diving into the Wreck."

190   **the thing I came for** Rich, "Diving into the Wreck."

206   **The (Carino) lived in the south** George S. Brown,
*Yarmouth, Nova Scotia: A Sequel to Campbell's
History*, (Boston: Rand Avery Company, 1888).

206   **With so many people** "An Acadian Parish
Reborn," Nova Scotia Archives, updated June
2024, https://archives.novascotia.ca/acadian
/reborn/families.

210   **Once they get into you** Rick Bass, *Wild to the
Heart*, reissue (New York: W. W. Norton, 1997),
88–89.

223   **in the Acadian land** "The Evangeline County,
Nova Scotia," Radford University: McConnell
Library, https://monk.radford.edu/records/item
/7252-the-evangeline-country-nova-scotia.

246   **To understand what** Joan Didion, *The White* Album
(New York: Farrar, Straus and Giroux, 1990), 83.

Acknowledgments

To my family—Dad, Kris, Kim—thank you for being on this journey with me through all its twists and turns and flat tires. Mom, you are so deeply missed in so many ways. Mike, I remain grateful for you bringing your family tradition of Reese's Peanut Butter Cups on s'mores into our family. To Cora, Henry, and Sam—being your Aunt Kinny is the best thing in my life, and I can't wait to make more memories Scamping with you.

This book would not exist without the keen eyes and sharp pens of Marya Hornbacher and Heidi Czerwiec, and I'm grateful to *Terrain.org* for publishing earlier versions of "Romer's Gap," to *Waxwing* for "Falling," and *Proximity* for "Beautiful Sun, in a Minor Key."

To my agent, Erik Hane, and the team at Milkweed—my deepest appreciation.

And in memory of Maeve (2007–2020) and Galway (2003–2021).

KAREN BABINE is the two-time Minnesota Book Award–winning author of *All the Wild Hungers: A Season of Cooking and Cancer* and *Water and What We Know: Following the Roots of a Northern Life* and the editor of *Assay: A Journal of Nonfiction Studies*. She is currently an UC Foundation Associate Professor of English at the University of Tennessee–Chattanooga.

milkweed
EDITIONS

Founded as a nonprofit organization in 1980, Milkweed
Editions is an independent publisher. Our mission is to
identify, nurture, and publish transformative literature, and
build an engaged community around it.

We are based in Bdé Óta Othúŋwe (Minneapolis)
in Mní Sota Makhóčhe (Minnesota), the traditional
homeland of the Dakhóta and Anishinaabe (Ojibwe)
people and current home to many thousands of Dakhóta,
Ojibwe, and other Indigenous people, including four
federally recognized Dakhóta nations and seven federally
recognized Ojibwe nations.

We believe all flourishing is mutual, and we envision a
future in which all can thrive. Realizing such a vision
requires reflection on historical legacies and engagement
with current realities. We humbly encourage readers to
do the same.

milkweed.org

Milkweed Editions, an independent nonprofit literary publisher, gratefully acknowledges sustaining support from our board of directors, the McKnight Foundation, the National Endowment for the Arts, and many generous contributions from foundations, corporations, and thousands of individuals—our readers. This activity is made possible by the voters of Minnesota through a Minnesota State Arts Board Operating Support grant, thanks to a legislative appropriation from the Arts and Cultural Heritage Fund.

Interior design by Mike Corrao

Typeset in Adobe Caslon Pro

Adobe Caslon Pro is a digital facsimile of William
Caslon's original 1722 typeface, inspired by the previous
century's Dutch type foundries. It was revived for
modern use in 1990 by the prolific Carol Twombly for
the Adobe Originals program.